Advance Praise for *Enablon and Me*

"*Enablon and Me* is a terrific story full of wisdom and great advice. Tom Barr describes a job change after being downsized and does so with an abundance of humor and wit. But this book is about much more than work—it is about embracing change, engaging with others, and trying to get the most out of each moment. Tom claims to be an old man, but his youth and enthusiasm come through loud and clear in this delightful book."

—James Lee, President, Onsight
(http://www.onsight.com/)

"If you like to read insightful business books that will have you alternating between mild chuckles and full out belly laughs, read this book. If your profession has you involved in international business, technical training, corporate training, consulting, or product advocacy, read this book a second time. You will have undoubtedly missed a subtle point or two as you were nodding, smiling, and laughing along with what you read the first time. And if you aspire to any of the aforementioned careers, read this book a third time to truly absorb its invaluable lessons."

—Martin Marks, Software Training
Development and Delivery Specialist

"A real-world story with no-frill tips from a successful business person. Told with humor and heart. What a terrific read."

—Corinne Miller,
founder of Innovating Results

"Tom Barr's stories about success and prosperity are told with humor and insight. His lessons apply in any organization where change is the norm and constant learning from experience is essential."

—Catherine Marienau, Ph.D., Professor,
Director of MA in Educating Adults Program,
Director of Center to Advance Education for
Adults, School for New Learning/DePaul

University, and Co-author of *Facilitating Learning with the Adult Brain in Mind* (2016)

"Tom provides precious business and working tips based on his wide experience, on how to face and manage working life changes, multicultural environments, and different styles of management, while keeping his remarkable kindness and devotion. This book is wise, honest, funny, and tender at the same time—very much like its author. Easy to read even for a French person like myself! I had the honor of being Tom's manager, but he actually turned out to be a true inspiration for me and the rest of my life and career."

—Angela Dal Molin, Entrepreneur

"In his entertaining book, *Enablon and Me,* Tom Barr takes you on a wild and wonderful adventure. You will be engaged from start to finish as you learn along with the author how to negotiate new cultures, technologies, and responsibilities beyond what you (or he) thought were humanly possible.

This is a great book for anyone who wants to keep the spirit of adventure and learning alive in their life and work."

—Pamela Meyer, Ph.D., Author of
The Agility Shift: Creating Agile and Effective Leaders, Teams, and Organizations

"How do you build a great organization that helps many of the world's largest and best-known companies reduce their impact on the environment, protect their employees, and contribute to a safer more livable planet? You start by hiring people who are passionate, smart, driven, ambitious, and most importantly, who are kind and compassionate. Tom is one of these people I have been lucky to recruit in my career. His life's lessons and his unique sense of humor will enlighten you."

—Phil Tesler, Entrepreneur and Investor focusing on companies making a positive impact on the world, and Co-founder of Enablon, the world's leading provider of Sustainability, EH&S and Operational Risk Management Technology

ENABLON AND ME

WHEN *THE* SUSTAINABLE SOFTWARE COMPANY
MET AN UNSUSTAINABLE OLD MAN

TOM BARR

Post Hill
PRESS

A POST HILL PRESS BOOK
ISBN: 978-1-64293-364-2
ISBN (eBook): 978-1-64293-365-9

Enablon and Me:
When the Sustainable Software Company Met
an Unsustainable Old Man

This is a work of nonfiction. All people, locations, events, and situations are portrayed to the best of the author's memory.

Post Hill Press
New York • Nashville
posthillpress.com

Published in the United States of America

For the woman who is my best friend,

always there with constant support, wisdom,

partnership, and love—my wife, Chris.

CONTENTS

INTRODUCTION

Although you have probably never heard of Enablon, and you certainly have never heard of me, I wrote this book to share lessons I have learned that I think can benefit you. You and I are likely very similar. I belong to several large demographic groups.

1. I am old (aka mature). Currently in the US, there are more than 108 million people over fifty.
2. I was unemployed in 2009. According to the results of a CNNMoney survey in March 2009, 12.5 million of us in the US were unemployed.
3. I joined a small company. The Small Business & Entrepreneurship Council tells us that in 2016 the United States Census Bureau reported that there were nearly six million businesses in the US and

that over 99 percent of these had fewer than five hundred employees.

4. I joined a company that was not US-owned. According to the Pew Research Center, in 2015 non-US-owned companies employed nearly seven million US workers.

Over my long career, I have had many colleagues seek my advice. Ever hear of Warren Buffett, Jeff Bezos, Tim Cook, Elon Musk, Larry Page, and Mary T. Barra? Well, I have heard of them, too (old joke). Nonetheless, I am a business success. I'm not bragging, because business success is not hard to achieve. It just requires reflection, planning, and follow-up. And that's what the insights and lessons throughout this book focus on—business success; how to achieve it if you haven't, and how to appreciate it if you have.

The key ingredient to business success is defining it—for you. Never mind how the media portrays success. What does success mean to you, on a personal level?

One dictionary definition of success is "that which achieves desired aims or attains prosperity." But this further begs the question: what are *your* desired aims and how do *you* describe prosperity? My definition of business success is composed of the following:

- Doing work which I enjoy, am enthusiastic about, and which is meaningful to me (in my case, which helps others).
- Having control of my work duties.
- Having opportunities to learn new things that interest me and contribute to my work.
- Being able to integrate my work life and non-work life such that neither detracts from the other.
- Enjoying fair compensation, substantial enough so that I have no money worries if I exercise sound spending practices.

It took a while to formulate this definition. I don't think my definition is unusual. In fact, Dan Pink, in his book *Drive, The Surprising Truth About What Motivates Us,* listed the top three items in my success definition as top motivators. More about Pink's book later.

I re-evaluate my success definition on a regular basis, gauge how aligned it is with my life, and take quick action if needed. For example, once this book gains unprecedented popularity, I will immediately add another bullet item to my success definition: engage countless readers worldwide with my keen written insights.

Similarly, if something goes counter to my definition or if my definition is off-balance or unrealistic, I take immediate action. When I finally realized that I could never make a living as a professional bowler (I had been profoundly motivated by Randy Quaid's performance in *Kingpin*), I quickly erased that item. Life is too short for weird definitions of success and for doing something that contradicts a solid definition.

The problem many people face is that they either haven't seriously or fully defined success or simply don't act to align their lives with their definition. In 2018, the Conference Board reported that 49 percent of Americans were dissatisfied overall with their jobs. Would these unhappy workers describe themselves as successful?

Adopting popular notions of success as our own success definition can be a disaster. A friend of mine aligned his notion of business success with the popular goal of making lots of money. He entered a profession that paid very well, but he hated what he did. He stayed at his job for nearly forty years and pretty much hated every minute of it. He earned lots of money, but was he really a success? In retrospect, he would be the first to admit that he was a victim of his own narrow, popularity-driven definition of success.

Some people bounce from one unhappy job to another. They realize their current employment is not fulfilling, but they don't plan carefully enough and end up in another job just as bad. They repeatedly make the same job-selection mistake because they don't map their job to a carefully-constructed definition of success.

In many ways they are like the guy with the severely burned ears. "What happened?" a friend asks him.

"The phone rang in the middle of the night. It was so dark, and I was so groggy, that I picked up a hot iron by mistake and held it to my ear."

"That explains one ear," says the friend, "but how did you burn the other?"

"The damn fool called back."

Or the worker who every day at lunch takes out her sandwich and complains, "Peanut butter and jelly *again*."

Every day. Peanut butter and jelly. *Again*.

A co-worker, noticing this, finally asks, "Why don't you ask your husband to make you another kind of sandwich?"

"Oh, I'm not married. I make my own sandwiches."

Are we burning our ears repeatedly and eating the same boring sandwich because we don't take the time to analyze our definition of success and take action?

Takeaway:

Ricky Nelson gave us solid business advice in his song "Garden Party." To paraphrase Ricky, since we can't make everybody happy, we at least should please ourselves—even those of us who don't attend garden parties because we're indoor people. And that is what success in business should do—it should please us, ultimately make us content and joyful, and provide meaning to our lives. But that success needs definition and nurturing.

CHAPTER **ONE**

THE INTERVIEW

I hesitated titling this chapter "The Interview," as I did not want it confused with that god-awful movie starring Seth Rogen and James Franco. But who am I to judge what is god-awful? As you read on, you may rate this chapter as even more god-awful—but at least (spoiler alert) there is no mention of Kim Jong Un.

Interviewing for a new job is a fine art. They say that practice makes perfect. In 2009, when I was part of a huge RIF (reduction in force—euphemism for being canned) at

Motorola as the aftermath of the great recession of 2008, I hadn't practiced in twenty-seven years. My definition of success was undergoing substantial evaluation.

The Galvin family (who, as the Galvin Manufacturing Corporation, founded Motorola in 1928) had, over the years, established a corporate culture of "family"—where employees were well taken care of (like members of a large family). But in 2008, I was being asked to leave the family because I had too many brothers and sisters, and mom and dad just couldn't afford us all anymore—and Uncle Carl (Icahn), the billionaire investor who had acquired millions of shares of Motorola stock and wanted to see greater profits from his investment, was creating a stir.

But even at my departure, I was still treated like family and given much support (both financial and moral). "There is life after Motorola" was a common saying among those of us who had left and thrived. (Those who had left and not thrived really didn't have a common saying.)

The Motorola name lives on but is often associated with a sold-off portion of the original (all that remains of the original, as of this writing, is Motorola Solutions).

I wasn't optimistic about my chances of landing another job. My life after Motorola would likely be retirement. I had sent out a hundred resumes and had only one interview—with a local university for a dead-end clerical position well below my expectations. And even there, they had me take an extensive online test and prepare a formal presentation to an "evaluation committee." I think I blew the job when, during the presentation, I showed a video representing my perception of the job: an old guy snoring in a recliner. Still, I thought I was more than qualified and was very disappointed when I learned I didn't get the job after all the hoops they had made me jump through.

I had skills—four degrees, including a PhD in software engineering, and twenty-seven years in various technical and management positions at Motorola. But, like many of my fellow unemployed colleagues, my experience automatically signaled higher salary demands. And, even if we came down in such demands—which everyone I knew did—employers thought, "How motivated will these people be if we underpay them? They'll only stay with us until they find something else."

So many of us, including me, wanting to prove our worth in this world of rejection, began seeking positions for which we were overqualified. This only made matters worse, for now employers could say, "How motivated will these people be in a non-challenging, low-paying job?" Some of my unemployed friends, in fact, became so desperate to find work, that they even lied about their experience and education to appear a better fit for more junior jobs.

It was September 2009 when I received a most uplifting email from our dear family friend Sister Carol, who had left the Chicago area several years earlier to work with young novice nuns in Africa. I had written her, describing how dejected I felt, having had so few job prospects. I will never forget her email reply, especially the last sentence:

> *Dear Tom,*
>
> *I'm very sorry to hear about the interview (or lack of) results.*
>
> *I was in a similar situation many years ago when, after 2 years in Congo, I stopped for 10 days in Nairobi, Kenya, to interview for a job as a pastoral minister in the slums working on a Team with 2 or 3 priests. I thought I did everything right, exactly as you described, only to find out when I got home that they would not hire me because of all kinds of reasons which I knew were not true. They wrote*

to our Team member, not even to me, and she wouldn't even share the letter with me. I was angry about this whole thing for 7 years. I later found out that what they were looking for was a sister to teach arts and crafts in the slums to replace a sister who had just returned to the U.S. Then why advertise for a sister to serve with priests as an equal on a pastoral team?

My learnings from this to apply to you: Just or unjust, there is nothing you can do. Probably, if they do give you any reasons at all, they will not be the real ones. In the end, it's all about money. In the end, I went to Nigeria 8 years later where I am really supposed to be and where I believe I have done an incredible amount of good for the Sisters here. I believe that at the end of it all, you too will find the place where you are to be; and it will be right. In the meantime, screw those people!

Love,
Carol

Takeaway:

Be yourself. Look for opportunities that align with your talents, expectations, and definition of success. Heed the words of a wise old nun: "...at the end of it all, you too will find the place where you are to be; and it will be right."

And then I got a call for an interview with a company with a strange name that was totally unknown to me. I had been well-coached in how to respond.

Motorola, as well as the state of Illinois, was instrumental in supplying programs in how to find a job for out-of-work, old and middle-aged, recently laid-off workers like me. We got all kinds of advice on how to excel at interviews. I soaked it all in.

- Dress up to show the importance you place on the potential job.
- Dress down because formal attire will make you look stuck-up and inflexible.
- Let the interviewer do as much of the talking as possible—less opportunity for you to say something stupid.

- Interject frequently into the conversation—it makes you appear engaged and interested in the position.
- Offer a firm handshake at both the beginning and the end of the interview.
- Let the interviewers take the lead on the handshake—they may be germophobic and wish to avoid your diseased skin.
- Maintain good eye contact with the interviewers throughout to establish a solid personal relationship.
- Avoid staring at the interviewers as they may think you are giving them the evil eye or are just basically weird.
- Research the hiring company thoroughly in advance and slip in some company facts into the interview to let the interviewer know that you have done your homework.
- Don't go out of your way to learn about the hiring company—let them tell you about it during the interview. You don't want to appear too eager and desperate.
- Bring multiple copies of your resume to the interview and hand them to the interviewers as a convenience to show your thoughtfulness.

- Don't bring copies of your resume to the interview. The hiring company already has a copy and it will only serve as a distraction during the interview.
- Use your job network—contacts in the industry—to help you with insights into the hiring company, the personnel, and the job itself.
- Avoid your job network—they will only give you biases that may jeopardize your interview and may even apply for the same position themselves.

Takeaway:
Advice is like money; you can never have too much, and though you don't have to use it all, better to have a wallet full of it than a near-empty purse.

Armed with this jumble of advice, in October 2009 I headed to the Willis Tower, in downtown Chicago, for my interview with Enablon. Many years later, as I watched Dwayne Johnson's blockbuster movie *Rampage,* in many ways I could relate to the giant albino gorilla, the giant winged wolf, and the giant alligator, all scaling the walls of the Willis Tower, on a mission to reach the top (or, in my case, the fifty-fourth floor). Like them, I was anxious and nervous (but at least I was spared the wrath of The Rock). I think I related best to the gorilla. He seemed like the one having the most fun.

- I felt totally unprepared for the interview. Of course, that may be regarded as a strong point depending on the interview advice you follow. I looked up Enablon online and found it described as a "Sustainability, EHS, & Operational Risk Management Software Company." In that description I could identify two words, "Software" and "Company." I also learned that the CEO was Philippe Tesler, by whom, I was told, I would be interviewed. One of the contacts in my job network had heard of him but had no details. Philippe, to me, was a mystery man. I wasn't even sure what to call him – Philippe, Philip, Phil, PT? Or was he a formal guy—Mr. Tesler (or maybe even *Dr.* Tesler)? And how should I pronounce Tesler? Did it end with the "er" sound or was it "ay" like "Teslay?" I decided to nod a lot and, if forced, to simply say "sir."
- I was interviewing for a job as "Knowledge Manager." I had never heard of this before. It sounded easy—all I had to do was manage knowledge. And it sounded

cool. What do you do for a living, Tom? Oh, I am a knowledge manager. We wouldn't want knowledge to go unmanaged now, would we? The formal definition of knowledge management (from Wikipedia) is "the process of creating, sharing, using and managing the knowledge and information of an organization. It refers to a multidisciplinary approach to achieving organizational objectives by making the best use of knowledge." What is this "multidisciplinary approach?" I was hoping Enablon could tell me.

- I wasn't even sure how to pronounce "Enablon" nor could I find out where the name exactly came from or what it meant. "Motorola" had come from "motor" (as in car) plus "ola" (from "Victrola", a record player company founded in the early 1900s)—meaning that Motorola put sound in cars by making car radios. Maybe Enablon enabled people online. Or maybe it was Mrs. Nolbane's last name spelled backwards. And were the "e," "a," and "o" long or short? I also found myself wanting to add an extra syllable—"En-able-on." I later found many Americans pronounce it that way. Surprisingly, there are few English words that end in "ablon"—just two, actually: "Ablon" (a

French commune in the Calvados Department, whatever that is, in the Normandy region in north-western France) and "Fablon" (a brand of adhesive-backed plastic material used to cover and decorate shelves, worktops, and so forth, and for handicraft purposes).

- I didn't have good vibes about the Willis Tower. It had just undergone a name change that year—2009. Previously it been called the Sears Tower and hadn't exactly been a good luck charm for Sears, Roebuck and Company. I knew the new name came from the Willis Group, an insurance broker, but I couldn't help thinking about Bruce Willis in the movie *Die Hard* with bloody feet chanting "Yippee-Ki-Yay" and swearing at the bad guys.
- The Willis Tower also reminded me of lawyers and that always terrifies me. Years earlier I had visited the Sears Tower as a Motorola software engineer to service a computer system for our client, Sears. I remember experiencing the ultimate nightmare—being surrounded by fifteen irate Sears' attorneys who used the system for their contracts and claimed it wasn't working. Being surrounded by attorneys is never fun, but I managed to quell their anger by

demonstrating that it was *their* IT staff who were using the system incorrectly and not a problem with the system itself. Still, I can never entirely erase the memory of those attorneys, so many of them glaring at me like Raymond Burr (who, you might recall, not only portrayed attorney Perry Mason but, on his dark side, was the creepy Lars Thorwald who dismembered his wife's body in Hitchcock's movie classic *Rear Window*).

- I am terrible with directions and it took me forever to reach the Enablon offices on the fifty-fourth floor—an elevator halfway up, then an escalator up one floor, then an elevator down thirty floors because I got on the wrong elevator, then back up, then the escalator again, then four or five more mistaken elevator rides up and down, a staircase or two, then all the way down to the front desk where one of the Tower's associates took pity on me and escorted me up to fifty-four.

I waited awhile in the small conference room for the interviews to begin. I didn't want to dress too up or too down so I wore a suit, but it was an old one. I didn't want my resume to distract, so I brought copies but wasn't handing them out until the end. I decided not to be too talkative. I could already feel stupid words, expressions, and sentences forming in my mouth.

Now from all this, you might think I am an idiot. When Laurie Harper, my friend and literary consultant, read this manuscript, she commented that my writing style has "...the 'I can't believe I succeeded' sound which can also come off as a fake golly gosh tone." To which I responded, "Well, golly gosh, I didn't intend that."

But the truth is, though I take my work seriously, I never take *myself* too seriously, and I enjoy poking fun at myself. If I didn't, I wouldn't be able to relax and have fun. I have encountered a few co-workers over the years who took themselves too seriously. They would always speak of themselves in the highest regard, without even a tinge of humorous self-deprecation. It was as though they were on guard to ensure that they continually cast themselves in the best light and beyond reproach.

Gustavo Razzetti, in his *Psychology Today* piece called "How to Stop Taking Yourself Too Seriously," states that when we take ourselves too seriously, "...We choose to look good over learning new things. Fear makes our lives boring and repetitive....Your image is not you. It's just what people perceive. Don't let your self-worth depend on your audience's applause. When your self-worth is not on the line, it's easier to take more risks and be courageous."

So, you see, I am not an idiot. I am courageous, golly gosh.

Takeaway:
Look at job interviews and important meetings as fun times. Don't take yourself so seriously. Like most people, you'll probably feel underprepared and worry about a million details, but if you come across as truly enjoying yourself, you'll shine—to others and, most importantly, to yourself.

Angela (pronounced "ahn-zhela," of course) was the head of the KM (acronym for knowledge management) team, all of whom worked at the Enablon headquarters in Paris. I was interviewing to become the first Enablon North American knowledge manager. She interviewed me before the CEO did. I think she was initially surprised by my age (I found out later that she is thirty years younger than I am). Of course, it's illegal to discuss age during an interview, but to break the ice, I told her I was a hundred. Then, when she nodded in acknowledgement, I told her I was only kidding.

Her English was excellent, though obviously accented in French. She pronounced "Enablon" in a French way that my limited tongue could not come close to imitating: "Eh—nay—bloh." Her questions were all about training and documentation. How much corporate training had I done—both internal and with clients? Had I developed any instructional materials and user guides? I was tempted to answer in French, but the only French words I knew were *"oui," "merci,"* and *"Maurice Chevalier"*—so I didn't want to start something I couldn't finish.

I also began to realize that, to Enablon, a knowledge manager was someone who did technical training and created documentation. This is what I had done for many years at Motorola, except there I was called a trainer. I like "knowledge manager" better. The term "trainer" always reminds me of either a sports trainer or an animal trainer, where I would be helping athletes, animals, or some combination thereof improve physical performance. Not that these aren't noble undertakings, but I prefer a title that denotes managing knowledge (whatever that means).

Midway through the interview, I realized I had been looking down too much. Between thinking about the "evil eye" interview advice and the glaring Sears' attorneys, I was freaking out about what to do with my eyes, so I instinctively looked down. Not a good idea, I told myself. Angela will think you are snoozing. So, for the remainder of the interview, I maintained eye contact, trying hard not to appear to be staring or making faces.

Angela, though born in Paris, has Vietnamese and Chinese roots. She is truly a citizen of the world as, I later discovered, are many of the Enablon employees, who, at that time, came from more than twenty-seven different countries. I, on the other hand, am a citizen of the northwest suburbs of Chicago. Where Angela frequents America, Europe, and Asia, I frequent Mount Prospect, Schaumburg, Arlington Heights, and Des Plaines, Illinois—and mostly just Mount Prospect, where I live.

Some older workers tend to talk down to younger colleagues, to exhibit their vast experience and knowledge of how things should be done the *right* way, the "been there, done that" attitude. That has never been my problem, for three reasons.

1. The groups I worked with at Motorola were never younger than I was. It wasn't unusual in Motorola's heyday to work with folks that had been with the company thirty-five, forty, even fifty years. I was a Motorola baby.
2. Even if I had encountered younger employees, I could never gloat over them on how to do things "the right way" because I am too humble for that. Granted, others who worked with me might replace "humble" with "ignorant." I prefer "humble."
3. And, though I had often probably "been there," I had usually not been clever enough to have "done that." But there I go, being humble again.

Takeaway:

Listen to others—truly listen, not trying to dominate the conversation with your perspectives. There is almost always something to be learned from others. As Anthony Liccione so aptly put it, "A fool is made more of a fool, when their mouth is more open than their mind."

Right from the start, Angela demonstrated to me that she was infinitely smarter and more skilled in all things Enablon than I could ever be. The passion and drive that Angela showed for her work was obvious and inspiring.

At the end of our interview, I was positive that I had at least convinced Angela of the following:

- I was old.
- My suit was old.
- I could look up.
- I knew Paris was in France.
- I could find the Enablon offices in the Willis Tower (with help).
- I had enjoyed a very solid career with Motorola before the great recession of 2008.

I had no idea whether this was enough to guarantee me a job. And even if I had passed the Angela test, final approval, I was sure, would depend on the CEO.

Who was this CEO? This Phil/Philippe Tesler? From the glass panels in the conference room where I was interviewed, I could see a bunch of guys in the corner office. One of them had to be the CEO, but which one? I had been unable to find any photo of Tesler online. He was truly a mystery man. I studied the guys in the corner office carefully after Angela left, trying to guess the real PT. The cast of characters was intriguing.

- Two very young dudes in T-shirts and tight jeans took turns pointing at a computer monitor and softly jabbered in what sounded like French. Each looked too young to be a CEO, but then again Mark Zuckerberg was only twenty-five in 2009.
- One very thin mid-thirtysomething guy stood at the keyboard. He was the man in black—black jersey, tight black jeans, and a black New York Yankees baseball cap. The other two seemed to be telling him what to type, so this surely wasn't CEO material.
- Another guy—in an untucked polo and jeans—bounced in and out of the office. Strangely, he resembled a young Raymond Burr...please, not him!
- The last candidate stood off to the side, taking it all in and occasionally adding a comment in what I guessed was French. He wore a navy suit jacket, slacks, and dress shirt. This was my choice for CEO. At Motorola, CEOs always seemed to dress up. Even

> informally, our last CEO from the Galvin Family—Chris Galvin—lost the suit jacket but still came nicely attired in impeccable dress pants and a monogrammed dress shirt, with cuff links.

Will the real Phil Tesler please step forward? It was... walking toward me...number three—the man in black. I was overdressed.

His accent was a bit thicker than Angela's. He offered a half-hearted handshake and the conversation went downhill from there. Trying to start off with friendly banter, I asked whether he preferred to be called "Philippe" or "Phil." He said he didn't care.

I mentioned that the company name—Enablon (pronounced in my Chicago accent)—was unique and asked where it originated. He said he wasn't sure. I found out later that he didn't want to describe the countless hours he and his co-founders had spent agreeing on a name, which came from the blending of the words "enable" and "on". Enablon software could "enable" collaboration between people and organizations as simply as flipping an "on" switch.

Then he began with a barrage of questions, each seemingly intended to put me ill at ease and make me dread the thought of even considering employment at Enablon.

- Was I aware that I would have to work long hours at Enablon?
- There was much travel involved. I would probably be traveling every week. Could I handle that?
- There were a lot of things to learn in a very short time. Did I think I was capable of picking things up quickly and on my own?
- He was aware that I had done technical training at Motorola—but that was some time ago. Did I think I could handle it now?
- Would I be willing to learn French? A lot of the documentation was already written in French and most of my co-workers, at least for now, spoke French as their primary language.

To each question, I enabled my "on" switch and answered with a resounding "Yes!" and then went on to pad each affirmation with enthusiastic and confident BS, for which, I have been told by many, I am quite skilled. He never cracked a smile or acknowledged any satisfaction with my answers. In fact, after each of my responses, he countered with "Yes, but..." trying to negate the validity of my answer.

Throughout the interview he appeared displeased, as if telling himself, "Why am I even talking to this fool?"

I thought I knew what he was doing but wasn't positive. My theory: He was testing my reaction to negative responses to determine how I might react to rejection from customers in the field. It was an old trick that I had used myself when interviewing folks at Motorola. I once got an interviewee so upset, she called me a jackass and stormed out of the office. When that happens, you only hope someone else at your company doesn't hire that person to be your boss.

A second half-hearted handshake from Phil/Philippe ended the interview, and I went home confident that I didn't get the job and that I didn't want the job. The next day I got a call with a job offer. If I accepted, I would start the following week at the Willis Tower office followed by two weeks in the Paris office for intense training. But did I want this job? Did I want to spend two weeks in Paris, the city that Hemingway called "a moveable feast" and of which Thomas Jefferson wrote, "A walk about Paris will provide lessons in history, beauty, and in the point of Life." I had never been to

Paris. Would I be going now—as an employee of Enablon—an "Enablonian?"

I could hear Dale Carnegie whispering in my ear: "Take a chance. All life is a chance. The man who goes farthest is generally the one who is willing to do and dare."

Takeaway:
Take a chance. Especially when it involves a meaningful challenge. And maybe a trip to Paris.

I look back at the interview with Phil as one of the major anomalies in my life. He is the Jekyll and Hyde of job interviews. With the prospective interviewee, dear sweet Phil Tesler Jekyll turned into the pugnacious Phil Tesler Hyde.

Others who have been interviewed by Phil have shared similar experiences. In one case, Phil never looked up from his laptop during the interview, firing challenging questions at the interviewee (a skilled sales rep named Ian, whom I later met in Paris) with no obvious response to any answer. At the end of the interview, with eyes still on his laptop, Phil said, matter-of-factly, "Okay, let's give this a try." Hardly a resounding "You're hired! Congratulations!"

Yet, as I look back at all the folks Phil has hired, I realize his interviewing technique is extremely effective because it catches people off guard and tests their innate ability to be amicable, flexible, and cool under pressure. These are traits not easily learned but vital to dealing with customers and co-workers and have been key to Enablon's success. Though, admittedly, I wish Phil would have ended our interview by jumping up and down and yelling, "You're hired! Congratulations!"

Takeaway:
The ability to be amicable, flexible, and cool under pressure will never let you down. Belligerent inflexible meltdowns are not good for business (or for life).

CHAPTER TWO

WORK BEGINS

When I departed in June 2009, Motorola (though it had taken its share of lumps) was still a mammoth organization. I worked primarily out of two Illinois offices—at the main campus in Schaumburg and at another in nearby Arlington Heights. Both facilities had multiple buildings with thousands of employees. At one time, it seemed everyone in the world worked for Motorola.

At its peak, I think the company had over one hundred and fifty thousand employees worldwide. When I told anyone I worked there, I would invariably get a response like, "Oh, my cousin Joe Shmuck works there, too. Do you know him?" The odds of me knowing Joe were more than remote, but I'd always say, "Joe. Sure. We've worked side-by-side for years, like brothers. And he's always talking about you...and what a jackass you are."

My snide "jackass" remark, I admit, really isn't fair or warranted because every once in a while it happens that the seemingly one-in-a-million long shot is right on. I reflected on long shots as I made my way to my first day at Enablon, an experience which seemed increasingly like a statistical anomaly. Unexpected coincidence, unanticipated surprises, sudden turns of events, seeing people you never expected to see—these are what make life exciting. What, after all, were the chances that an old software guy from a large, well-established American company would be working for a small, young French company with a job title he had never heard of? Hopefully, my experience would be an enriching twist of fate—like winning the lotto or finding a long-lost friend—and not a bad one like having an errant pigeon poop directly on my head.

Takeaway:

Don't discount coincidence and the unexpected. There is a connectedness of humans and of life in general that often seems unfathomable but that highlights our oneness. It was by mere chance that I found this quote by musician Alva Noto, "There is always room for coincidence." But beware of pigeons.

George H. W. Bush, when he was president, had once visited our Motorola Schaumburg campus. I remember standing on the huge field between buildings with thousands of other Motorola employees watching four Air Force helicopters slowly descend onto the campus. Bush rode in one of them, but there was never any indication of which one it was (some friends and I secretly took bets) until they all landed, and he got out, surrounded by guards and under the watchful eyes of the sharpshooters who were positioned on the roofs of all the nearby buildings.

On my first day at Enablon at its Willis Tower offices, I thought of the vastness of Motorola and Bush's visit. After a few false starts not unlike my first visit to the office, I made it to the fifty-fourth floor on my own. I rounded the corner of the conference room where I had been interviewed the previous week. I had not seen this part of the office before, not even a glimpse. I was sure our new president, Barack Obama or the French president, Nicolas Sarkozy, had never even heard of Enablon, so I doubted they would be stopping by to say "hi" as George H. W. had at Motorola. Nor did I expect to see thousands of Enablonians busily at work in an endless maze of cubes. But I wasn't quite prepared for what I did see: a half-dozen guys sitting around a table preoccupied with their laptops in an otherwise empty room. This was it? Enablon North America Corporation?

I didn't even see Phil or Angela, but young Raymond Burr was there. And the two other young dudes who had been pointing at the monitor. Introductions were a blur. A few more people sat around a table in an adjoining office. And, I was told, some other employees—sales reps—either worked from home or were on the road. I was shown to another adjoining office. For now, I would be the sole occupant; after all, I was *the* knowledge manager.

It didn't take me long to realize, however, that I had little knowledge of what I was supposed to manage and that no one in the Chicago office really knew what I was supposed to do (except for Phil and Angela, who weren't there). I spent the week filling out new hire paperwork, experimenting with the

Enablon software, and reading existing documentation, most of which was in French with some interspersions of English or a mixture of French and English referred to as "Franglish," also sometimes called "Franglais." I found the following especially interesting in the Enablon use of English—so much so, in fact, that I began to favor the Enablon/French way—et began to incorporate their expressions in my own speech et writing.

- They put an "s" at the end of English plural words that didn't use the "s" to show plurality. Prime examples: "equipments" and "feedbacks."
- Pronouncing "idea" like "ID." When I was asked, "What is your ID?" I confused the requestor by taking out my driver's license.
- Pronouncing "demo" like "deemo," which I initially related to something demonic or frenzied (and which it probably was if I was giving it).
- Use of "precise" for "specify"—for example, "This attribute may be precised this way...."
- Use of "edition" for "editing"—for example, "This functionality is used for addition, deletion, and edition of a record."

- The ever-present word "requetor"—which I still haven't figured out completely, but I guess is a combination of "request" and "inquiry."
- The use of the French "*et*" for "and" in an otherwise completely English sentence.
- The use of "propose" immediately followed by the person to whom you are making the proposal—as in "I propose you that we should do this."
- Using obsolete words to represent modern English equivalents. Instead of using "observer," for example, Enablon used "observator" (though, personally, I think "observator" sounds cooler and makes more sense; after all, we call a room with an astronomical telescope to observe the universe an OBSERVATORy, not an OBSERVERatory).

I also initially butchered the names of the French guys in the office. Arnaud I mispronounced "Ar-nod" and not the correct "Ar-no." Clement, to me, was "Clement," not "Clem-o." I called Camille "Cam-eel" instead of "Cam-ee," which I thought was a nickname, so in emails, I started calling him "Cammy" until he set me straight. I also learned the difference between "*Francois*" (Fran-swa), male, versus "*Francoise*" (Fran-swaz), female. When confused, I just called them "Fran."

Folks in the office originally called me "Thomas" (Toe-ma), until I told them I preferred "Tom," which in French is "*Matou*." Eventually, they just called me "TBarr" or, sometimes, "*le vieil homme*." I figured out that "*le*" is "the" and "*homme*" is "man" and that "*vieil*" must be "great" or "wonderful" or "kind." If it does mean something else (which now I strongly suspect), I prefer not to know.

Sometimes, my French co-workers would be talking to me in English, then abruptly change to French, cutting me out of the conversation completely. I honestly believe this language switch was inadvertent. They simply reverted to the language to which they felt most comfortable. Still, I found it irritating and sometimes couldn't help but wonder whether they were talking about me and didn't want me to know.

To get even, sometimes when I was talking to them, I would throw in a word like "bolubba" or "zalapama." When they looked at me bewildered, I would respond, "Oh, that's a Chicago term. Aren't you familiar with it?" I got evil satisfaction from my little joke, until one day one of the French guys told me, "You need to check your bolubba."

"Huh?" I had forgotten my previously used nonsense word.

"Your bolubba—you know what that means right? After all, you are from Chicago."

Touché (another French word)!

Ron, one of our American sales reps, feared that US clients might balk at doing business with Enablon if it appeared too "foreign." Consequently, he had me join several client calls (even though I had little to contribute) because I had a very American-Chicago accent. And, in communication with clients, Ron magically adjusted the names of the Enablon team. Emmanuel, for example, became "Manny" and Cyril became "Chuck." And our CEO was always Phil, never Philippe.

As I adjusted to the Enablon world, I was confident everything would become much clearer once I got to Paris and underwent the intense training. There was a tight timeline, I discovered, because a week after my return from Paris, I was already scheduled to deliver hands-on software training to a customer in Denver.

Things were moving fast. I would surely be challenged. But, strangely, I was beginning to like this gig and was getting enthused about the whole thing. I recalled the quote from the esteemed Winston Churchill: "Success consists of going from failure to failure without loss of enthusiasm." I was sure I could move enthusiastically from failure to failure. What I wasn't sure about was whether Enablon viewed this as success. Well, at least Churchill did.

Takeaway:

Listen to Churchill: Success always involves new, unknown factors and failures, but it is driven by enthusiasm.

CHAPTER THREE

WELCOME TO PARIS

Enablon headquarters filled all floors of a six-story building on Boulevard Georges Clemenceau, north of the Seine River. Enablon had started, I was told, with one floor, and as the company grew, eventually took over the whole building. I think that was their strategy in moving to the Willis Tower. Start on one floor—the fifty-fourth—then eventually take over all 110.

I was staying at the tiny Hotel Hermes just across the Seine. I felt aligned to this hotel as soon as I saw its name;

Hermes, after all, was the Greek messenger of the gods, just as I would be the knowledge messenger of Enablon. Of course, maybe this was a stretch because Hermes was also god of animal husbandry, and I wasn't planning on breeding any farm animals—but you never know.

The Enablon Paris office taught me a lot about Enablon and about the French, some of which I was even able to retain.

They wanted me to feel at home and to meet as many Enablon employees as soon as possible, because, after all, I would be helping to manage their knowledge. When Angela said she was going to introduce me to my fellow Enablonians in Paris, I had no idea that meant she was immediately taking me to each of the six floors to introduce me to everyone, including two of the three co-founders of the company (besides Phil): the Vogel (pronounced "Vo-zhel") brothers, Dan and Marc.

I met over a hundred people in under an hour. I am bad with names and worse with French names I cannot pronounce—not that everyone was French. Diversity was a key corporate principle from the onset of the company, and Enablon proved a vast melting pot of people of all colors and origins—but they all seemed to speak French, except me.

Years later, when talking with Enablonians from Paris, I would say, "So glad to meet you." And they would respond that we had already met...during my whirlwind introduction binge with Angela. It was surely easier for them to remember me—an old, confused-looking American—than for me to remember the endless sea of young French-speaking faces I had encountered on my first day in France. Then I would go into BS mode (so as not to make them feel forgotten) and say, "Oh, silly me, of course I remember you—it's coming back to me now. Vividly! How could I forget *you*?"

It didn't take long for me to discover that if you didn't get along with people and have an upbeat attitude, you didn't last long at Enablon. Another new hire, who was also staying at Hotel Hermes, was a German guy named Ingo. To me, he looked like an Ingo—a big, burly fellow, with short hair and a large, square jaw, who reminded me of a henchman in a James Bond movie, where the main villain snarls, "Ingo, beat up Mister Bond!"

Unfortunately for Ingo (and for those of us around him), Ingo acted like a henchman. He complained vigorously from day one about pretty much everything and everyone—the laptop he had been given was no good, the introductory training we were receiving was inadequate, the work facilities (and

Hotel Hermes) were dreadful, and the Enablon approach to business was deficient. Within a very short time, Ingo was Ingone. Phil had obviously not interviewed him.

Takeaway:
Nobody likes a complainer; they never end up well, either in business or in a James Bond movie.

I experienced a French work time (at least at Enablon and, I suspect, in general) that differed greatly from what I was used to. When I arrived between 7:00 and 8:00 a.m., I was usually alone in the office; others trickled in starting at 9:00 a.m., and we reached the full workforce somewhere around 11:00 a.m. But while I was ready to head for the door by 4:30 p.m., the late arrivers stayed until very late at night. This prompted me to compose a short poem:

Early to bed,
Early to rise,
Doesn't work well
For the Enablon French guys.
Come in by mid-morning
And work very late

And you'll produce software

That works really great!

Angela admitted she had rarely ever eaten dinner before 9:00 p.m., a time when I was usually brushing my teeth and slipping into my jammies. The Enablon late-night culture is best represented by what happened months later, after I had returned from Paris. Angela visited me in the Chicago office and suggested we go out to dinner with some co-workers. Of course, it would be a late dinner. It was getting late for me when she asked—4:30 p.m.—and I was already sleepy and hungry but wasn't about to refuse my boss. So I kept busy, fought off exhaustion, and tried to silence my hollow, rumbling stomach.

Phil was busy meeting with two other Enablonians, and Angela invited all three of them to join us. It was approaching 8:30 p.m. Phil told us to go and that he and the other two would join us shortly. We settled in at the restaurant and kept texting Phil to see when he was coming. He kept delaying. Finally, by 9:30 p.m. we ordered and ate. Phil was still delaying. As we enjoyed dessert, Phil finally confirmed that he and the other two weren't coming. The next morning, I asked the two who had been meeting with Phil whether they had eventually gone to dinner—and where. Their meeting hadn't ended till after 1:00 a.m. No restaurants were open, so they all went to bed hungry.

Come in by mid-morning
Late through the day meet.
But if Phil is involved
Just remember to eat.

Though Enablon's French employees (and I suspect French companies in general) work hard and late, they also take time to relax and have fun. I saw nobody in the Paris office bring lunch to their desk and nibble while working through lunchtime. Work areas were wide-open, with everyone facing each other and no cube privacy, so eating at one's desk was disruptive to others, especially if, like me, you made distracting eating-related sounds, spilled crumbs all over, and ate pungent foods.

Everybody went out for a leisurely lunch—late, sometimes well after 1:00 p.m.—but leisurely, because when they returned, they still had another six or seven hours remaining in their workday. Fridays were the exception, when folks headed for home (or a nearby bar) usually by five or six. I am a get-to-work-early, eat-disgustingly-at-your-desk, work-through-lunch, leave-work-early kind of guy, so this change in work schedule was extremely hard for me to get used to as a new hire at Enablon.

The fun excursions during non-work hours helped compensate for my change in work schedule. To better acquaint me with my KM co-workers in Paris, Angela planned some enjoyable after-work activities for us. Everyone on the team spoke English (some better than others) and everyone spoke French, except me. We did lots of stuff.

- We had dinner at a quaint bistro. The tables were very close together with open seating for patrons to settle in wherever they wished. I spoke for nearly ten minutes with a member of the KM team whom I had not met before and who spoke excellent English...until Angela finally told me that he was a total stranger who just happened to sit with our group.
- We saw the Voca People (who resemble the Blue Man Group except in white face), who sing mostly in English and try to imitate the sounds of an entire orchestra, though I thought they struggled a bit in trying to sound like the contrabass balalaika. After

the performance, we took a group photo at the theater marquee. How appropriate: We were the Voca People of Enablon—an orchestra of knowledge with Angela as our conductor, and I was sure I would sing many raw notes along the way.

- We took a nighttime cruise of the Seine on the *Bateau Mouche*—which literally means boat (*bateau*) fly (*mouche*). I thought I was getting the hang of French, as I almost immediately identified "*bateau*" as "boat." But then there was "*mouche*." Fly? Really? Maybe it was distantly related to what the Arctic explorers yelled to drive their dog sleds—"Mush"—but this, I think, is more related to the French "*marché*" (meaning "walk"—to get the dogs moving, but not flying). Honestly, did a Frenchman, to avoid embarrassment, ever glance down at his pants to see whether his *mouche* was open? Anyhow, the *Bateau Mouche* took us past the Eiffel Tower, Notre Dame Cathedral, the Louvre, the Orsay Museum, and the tiny replica of the Statue of Liberty. The moon was in full view and resembled the head of a giant Voca Person happily shining down on us.

- We enjoyed an evening at an outdoor café, sipping wine and watching the lights of the Eiffel Tower flash for five minutes on the hour.

Angela also took great pains to ensure that I could enjoy Paris on the weekend. She showed me a tourist website (in French) and helped me book a city tour of Paris, online. The tour bus was to pick me up at a certain hotel at 9:00 a.m. sharp on Saturday. I left Hotel Hermes at 7:00 a.m. to be sure I would arrive at the pickup point on time, considering my horrible sense of direction. Nine a.m. came and went and no tour bus. I spoke to the hotel concierge, who phoned the tour company and spoke to them in frantic French. It seems they had never received my online booking...but I could still catch up with the tour at Notre Dame Cathedral if I immediately grabbed a taxi (which the concierge helped me flag down and explained to the driver, in French, where to take me).

Notre Dame Cathedral is huge. I hurriedly surveyed every street surrounding it. No sign of a tour bus or even a tour group. My taxi had left, and I was stuck. Then I spotted a bright red hop-on/hop-off double-decker city tour bus. I jumped aboard, paid my twenty-three Euros, received a cheap headset that I plugged into the outlet marked "English" on the upper level, and listened to narration of each stop we made. The ride was so much fun, I stayed on for two loops of Paris.

I couldn't help but compare my situation to that of the average Enablon customer. I had a definite plan to work with a more complex and costlier alternative (my original online tour company), but they failed me, and I was lost. Then, out of nowhere, to the rescue came the bright red bus (Enablon) offering me a much less expensive alternative that turned out so much easier and more rewarding than I could have ever hoped. As I further considered my analogy, I thought, "To-ma, are you becoming Enablonized, or what?"

Takeaway:

Embrace new people, new cultures, new companies that come your way—they add meaning to your life by opening new possibilities for more to learn and more to love.

During that four-month period between Motorola and Enablon, when I wasn't applying for jobs or attending seminars on how to land another job, I was at the Mount Prospect Public Library, which proved a much-needed job search diversion. The library had many enriching programs, one of which was entitled "How to Publish and Sell Your Book" by a local author with the last name of Bartholome. His presentation was quite interesting but focused on his experiences in publishing and selling his coffee table books. My interest, in contrast, was how to produce a blockbuster nonfiction business-related book (like this one). Anyhow, I chatted with him briefly afterwards, and he mentioned he would be traveling to Paris within the next couple of months to promote his books internationally. He even mentioned, off-hand, the hotel where he would be staying. Hold that thought.

When I arrived in Paris, I had considerable cash in US dollars, and some Euros that I had obtained at my currency exchange in Chicago. But my leisurely lunches, dinners, and sightseeing were depleting my Euros. I had a credit card, but many of my purchases were at such tiny establishments that credit cards weren't accepted. I needed more Euros. Normally, in the few overseas trips I had taken for Motorola, the hotel contained a currency exchange, where I could easily convert my dollars. But tiny Hotel Hermes didn't provide such a service. There were no easily-accessible currency exchanges and nearby banks didn't provide the service either.

Now I know what you are thinking. Don't you have an ATM debit card, fool? Answer: No. Somehow, I had gotten through life—and sparse international travels—never needing one.

So, I tried a larger hotel nearby. The front desk manager was happy to accommodate me. "And what is your room, sir?" he asked, as a follow-up.

"Oh, I don't have a room here. I'm at the Hotel Hermes and they don't provide currency exchange there."

"Oh, Hermes." He looked at me in pity. "Sir, I am sorry. We only provide this service to our guests. Perhaps you could use an ATM? There are many in the area."

I shrugged and walked away, embarrassed to say I didn't have a debit card. I could almost hear him mumbling "imbecile" under his breath. But I didn't give up. I returned a few hours later and took a quick look at the front desk. The next shift had reported for work, so I plopped down my US dollars and asked the woman behind the desk as sweetly as possible for Euros.

"And what is your room number, please?"

Time for my clever lie. "I'm sorry. I don't remember. My wife went out sightseeing earlier and took the key card with the room number."

"No worries. What is your name?"

Now I was nervous. I covered my hand with my mouth, as if concealing a cough, and murmured, "Baaaaaaaaaaaarrrrrrrrrrrrrr."

"Ah, Mister Bartholome?"

"Exactly." And it hit me immediately that this was the place the coffee table book guy from the Mount Prospect Public Library had said he would be staying. Coincidence! Little did I think back then that I would be masquerading as him to get my dollars converted to Euros. After the exchange, she had me sign a form, on which I scribbled illegibly, and the deed was done. I often wonder whether he ever found out and whether he ever sold any of his coffee table books internationally.

Takeaway:
You haven't really lived until you do something harmlessly sneaky—emphasis on *harmlessly*. You'll have a cool, humanizing story to tell and re-tell and maybe even write about (perhaps in a coffee table book).

In addition to the leisurely lunches, cozy bistros, Voca People sing-alongs, Seine cruises, wine sipping, red bus rides, and coffee book author masquerading, there was, of course, work. That work, for me, meant acquiring and mastering the copious pieces of knowledge that I would be tasked with managing.

The first thing I learned (informally) was the history of Enablon. It gave me a strong and uncanny feeling of *déjà vu* (a French word, after all).

- Enablon had been started in 2000 by two brothers, Dan and Marc Vogel, and their friend Phil Tesler, who had previously been working for software companies during the dot-com boom; together, they decided to start their own software company.
- Twenty-seven years earlier I was hired by a small computer company called Four-Phase Systems, started in 1968 by a guy named Lee Boysel (almost rhymes with Vogel), who had worked for Fairchild Semiconductor before deciding to strike out on his own. When I was hired by Four-Phase in April 1982, I had no idea that the company had just been acquired by Motorola the month before.
- Marc Vogel, the technical genius behind Enablon, created a software platform that enabled users

to easily interact with databases through a web browser, thereby reducing their reliance on multiple, complex, difficult-to-manage spreadsheets.

- Lee Boysel, the technical genius behind Four-Phase Systems, developed computers, computer terminals, and easy-to-use software for clients, thereby reducing their reliance on difficult-to-manage computer keypunch machines.
- At the heart of Marc Vogel's software design was something called the Application Server, on which multiple applications could reside to interface with a database and numerous other network services.
- At the heart of Lee Boysel's software design was IDOS (the Interrupt Disk Operating System), which later evolved into MFE (the Multi-Function Executive) on which multiple applications could reside.
- The first Enablon software application was called Metrics, which allowed clients to create their own forms that could be used for data collection and reporting.
- The first Four-Phase software application was called Vision, which allowed clients to create their own forms for data entry, replacing keypunch machines.

- When I was hired by Four-Phase/Motorola, I immediately was sent for extended training in exotic Dallas, Texas—Big D.
- As a newly hired Enablonian, I was sent for extended training in exotic Paris, France—the City of Lights, la Ville Lumière. I was trading my cowboy hat for a beret, and my "Howdy, partner" for "Salut."

It seemed the biggest difference for me, in starting out with Four-Phase twenty-seven years earlier, was that now, in training clients onsite, I no longer had to lug a whole computer system (including terminals) with me because all that was needed with Enablon were laptops (or tablets), an internet connection, and a browser. Where Four-Phase computers acted as an intermediary collection point from which data was ultimately uploaded to a "mainframe" computer for processing, Enablon users were interacting directly with the "mainframe" via their internet browsers. But users were still entering data and looking for the most user-friendly ways to do so. So, as they say, "the more things change, the more they stay the same"—or, in other words, "*Plus les choses changent, plus elles restent les mêmes.*"

Takeaway:

The older we become, the more things seem to repeat in cycles—almost like Bill Murray's character in *Groundhog Day*. That repetition strangely brings order to our view of the world and often predictability as well, for while technology changes, human nature somehow remains the same. There is great wisdom in old age (I am biased).

Dan Vogel served as the CEO of the entire Enablon company—for both Europe and North America. His specialty was business, aligning everyone to best meet the needs of Enablon and its customers. Marc, as I mentioned, was the technical guru. It seemed to me that he viewed the business part of Enablon as the necessary evil to allow him to devote full time to his passion—software development. Dan and Marc, therefore, were perfect complements to each other—Enablon's dynamic duo.

And then there was Phil. The CEO of Enablon North America Corporation as well as the leader of Enablon's global business development, global marketing, global partnerships, analyst relations, and global product organization.

Phil was the "Renaissance Man" of Enablon—technically adept and savvy in business. His true passion, however, was marketing and client interaction, winning the tough client, communicating in a way most appealing to the broadest audience. This was what motivated his "tough guy" interviewing technique. He wanted to hire only people who could be as charming and resilient as possible in the face of adversity. I don't know that I ever thought of myself as charming and resilient, but if that worked for Phil, I could go with it. At least I could try to appear charmingly resilient or, at least, resiliently charming.

As Enablon's client base expanded to North America, many in the Paris office found themselves frequently traveling to the US and Canada. This travel got so out of hand that in 2008 the company decided to establish a second headquarters in North America. Like a modern-day Jacques Cartier, Phil volunteered to lead the Enablon expedition. With two American-born guys who were living in France—sales reps Ron and Drew—and a half-dozen French software engineers, Phil began the exploration.

The timing could not have been worse. The great recession of 2008 was rearing its ugly head. Like many historic explorations, there were times when the group felt like abandoning their journey and returning home. But they persisted. They chose Chicago, with its central location to the US and Canada, as its base of operations. Headquartered initially in a modest hotel room, the team slowly but surely expanded operations until, by 2009, the Willis Tower seemed a likely home where they could begin hiring additional locals—like me.

Speaking of timing, one day Angela confided in me that my Enablon job interview had come at the most fortuitous time, as she had just happened to be in the Chicago office to help with "ENUF" earlier that week.

"Enough of what?" I replied.

"ENUF."

"Of what?"

This went on for a few minutes, our version of Abbot and Costello's "Who's on First?" ENUF, it turns out, stood for the Enablon North American Users Forum, a conference of Enablon clients and prospects where Enablon software was highlighted and discussed. I would have called it ENAUF, but how exactly do you pronounce that? There was also an EWUF. No, not a character from Warcraft. The Enablon Worldwide Users Forum held in Paris. Most of the clients who attended EWUF were Europeans, so perhaps the Enablon European User Forum, or EEUF, would have been more suitable, though saying it sounds too much like a sneeze. But was EWUF—which sounded (at least when I said it) like a bad imitation of a dog barking—any better?

The names ENUF and EWUF never really caught on (though rumor has it that one client used the names for her twin gerbils) and eventually were changed to SPF followed by the name of the venue. Sustainable Performance Forum—SPF Americas, SPF EMEA (Europe, Middle East, Africa), SPF Houston, SPF Australia, SPF Calgary, and so forth. We have had over a dozen of these gatherings of clients in Enablon's history—but to avoid confusion with sun protection we have avoided numbers, as in SPF 15.

It was very helpful to learn the informal beginnings of Enablon, but the real learning was technical and intense. Innumerable forms, workflows, usage rules, configuration tools and settings, data formats—even a proprietary programming language. Not very difficult stuff, just lots of it condensed into a very tight time frame. My head was swimming—in the Seine.

One evening, after a long day, I stared at my laptop in my room at the Hotel Hermes, trying to force myself to learn and retain more knowledge, when a message flashed on the screen. From Phil. "How is it going?"

"Wonderful!" I responded. "Lots to learn!"

"Are you learning any French yet?"

"*Oui.*"

That was a mistake, because Phil's next response was a paragraph entirely in French. I tried to decipher quickly, typing frantically into Google Translate, but I probably mis-typed some words because the results were "The water in the ditch is swimming with chewy eyeballs." I didn't think this was what Phil was saying. So, I responded in English, "I am not that good at French yet. It will take time. But I will avoid swimming in the ditch."

"Good luck with your studies."

I wanted to respond with "*Merci*" but feared that might spark another French exchange that would once again reveal my Google Translate deficiencies. But I didn't want to say "Thanks" either since Phil would think me an idiot for not even knowing enough French to respond "*Merci.*" So I did what I have grown accustomed to when at translation cross-roads. I sent Phil the smiley face emoji. I love the smiley face and use it frequently, both the emoji and the real one at the front of my head.

CHAPTER FOUR

GREAT CEOs

This brief encounter with Phil demonstrated, yet again, something I have noticed about great CEOs. Granted, I hadn't had much interaction with many CEOs, basically just Phil and Bob Galvin and his son Chris. What makes them truly great, I think, is that they appreciate the importance of others, regardless of how insignificant or lowly they are in the organization, like me.

Phil didn't have to take the time to message me. When I returned to the Chicago office, he would go out of his way to say "Hi" ("*Salut*") or wave or ask how I was doing. Once, when my son came to visit, he motioned for us to come into his office, even though he was in the middle of an important meeting. He stopped everything for a moment just to meet my son and find out how he liked visiting Enablon. It's little things like this that employees remember and tell their friends and co-workers again and again. CEO stories. Little motivating treasures. Everyone at Enablon had a Phil story. Of course, in our Chicago Willis Tower office, that wasn't hard to imagine, as we started out with only about a dozen employees.

And then there was the cap story. I was visiting a client on the West Coast with my Enablon associate Richard ("Rishard"). The client sold sports-related apparel and allowed us to shop at their onsite store, which provided substantial employee discounts. Richard loaded up with goods, and, with a sparse amount of luggage, ended up flying back to Chicago with his purchases tucked everywhere possible, including gym shoes stuffed into his pants pockets. I was more moderate, but noticed a black sports cap, soft and comfy, with the client logo on the front. Perfect for Phil. I bought it for him.

Upon my return to Willis Tower, noting that Phil was in his office, I messaged him, "Can I see you?"

He was thrown by my abruptness. "Now?"

"Yes. It will be brief."

I think he suspected I had bad news for him. Really bad news—like a client was threatening to terminate its license agreement. *Or* moderately bad news—like a client was upset with us. *Or* sort of bad news but maybe not really that bad—like I was going to quit. He hesitated for a few minutes, then responded, "Ok."

I went to his office, plopped down the cap, and said, "I saw this at the client's employee store and thought you might like it."

He thanked me but didn't say much else—until later in the day when he told me that he liked the cap so much that he had gone online to buy five more just like it. And he wore that cap every day for the rest of the week. In retrospect, I'm very glad I didn't buy him the alternative gift—a gag gift I had considered, a multicolored beanie with a propeller on top with huge red letters that said, "Look at Me."

At Motorola, what blew me away was the number of employees who had Bob Galvin stories. Bob was CEO of Motorola for twenty-seven years (from 1959 to 1986) with an employee count that at one time well exceeded one hundred thousand. Yet every employee I ever met seemed to have a Bob story. Bob invited one employee to his estate, so Bob could teach him how to windsurf on the Galvin's private lake. Bob asked another employee to investigate why Bob's wife's Motorola car phone suddenly wasn't working; it turned out Bob forgot to pay the phone bill.

My own Bob story happened when commemorative books about Motorola history were being distributed and signed by Bob. I was unable to attend, but a friend of mine went and mentioned to Bob that another employee (me) was unable to come due to a previous work commitment. Bob asked my name and graciously signed a copy of the book for me, thanking me in his note by name for my service to the company. Unfortunately, his thanks started with "Dear Don." So, either my friend said the wrong name on purpose as a joke or he had another friend named Don whom he liked better than me and figured I wouldn't want the book and would give it back to him, so he could give it to Don. *Or* maybe Bob was hard of hearing or my friend mumbled my name or both. *Or* maybe Bob had sloppy handwriting and his cursive "T" looked like "D" and "m" looked like "n." I'd like to believe the last case as I still have the book. At least the "o" looks good.

Chris Galvin was like his dad, and though he wasn't CEO as long as Bob, folks seemed to have Chris stories as well. I do. After a trip to China, I sent Chris an email thanking him for the opportunity. At that time, most American companies were shying away from China, but I thought it was a significant opportunity to share both business and culture and bring the world closer together. I never thought he would respond, but he did, thanking me for my efforts and not calling me Don.

I regret that I do not have a Lee Boysel story. Lee had departed Four-Phase Systems after it was acquired by Motorola and I was hired. I don't believe I was in any way responsible for his leaving. Many Four-Phasers who had worked for the company prior to its acquisition had marvelous Lee stories, from the humble beginnings of the company in what was literally a garage in 1968, to its growth as a major corporation over the next fourteen years with thousands of employees.

A contemporary of Lee Boysel, and like Lee, a pioneer in computing and software, was Dennis Ritchie. Dennis never became a CEO, yet his accomplishments in software—including the C programming language and the Unix operating system—certainly qualified him. At the time of his retirement in 2007, he was head of the Systems Software Research Department at Lucent Technologies, a spin-off of

AT&T. I mention Dennis here because he had a great CEO-mindset that he demonstrated so magnificently during my brief encounter with him.

I admit it. I was a Dennis Ritchie groupie. My daily work life in my middle years at Motorola was driven by the Unix operating system and by the C language. The brief book describing the language, *The C Programming Language*, by Ritchie and his colleague Brian Kernighan, became my software bible. While others could recite chapter and verse of the Good Book, I could reference page and paragraph of *The C Programming Language*. To us devotees, the book was simply K&R. Kernighan and Ritchie, the two geniuses of C.

When Dennis came to visit Motorola, I was excited. I, with a few dozen others, would actually get to meet him. *And* he would be available to sign books afterwards. I have always regretted missing the Bob Galvin signing ("Don!"), so I wasn't about to miss Dennis. The signing was a BYOB (bring your own book) so I quickly grabbed one of his books (my C bible was not handy) and rushed to the meeting.

I remember standing in line, anxiously awaiting my chance to meet this living legend, shake his hand, thank him for all his groundbreaking work, and ask him to sign my book. Moments seemed like hours...then, finally, my turn came. I shook his hand. I thanked him. I handed him my book and...as the book left my hand and slid into his...I realized...the book I was handing him to sign was...*The Practice of Programming* by Brian Kernighan. My obsession with K&R had been so great that I had failed to distinguish K from R. Dennis's hand was already on the book, so I couldn't pull it away. He asked my name. I told him. Nervously, I wondered what he would do.

I smiled at him sheepishly as he returned the book and I hurried on my way, eager to see what he had written. What a gentleman! Thinking of the little, insignificant guy (me), creating win-win situations, and reacting quickly but so elegantly to the stupid acts of others (me again). Maybe Dennis Ritchie wasn't a CEO, but he probably could have been one had he wanted to—he sure had the qualities of a great one, at least in my book (even though it turned out to be the wrong book).

> *Dear Tom,*
> *Wishing you much success,*
> *Dennis Ritchie (for Brian Kernighan)*

I still have the book. I tell the story often.

Phil stories, I realized, would be more limited. Enablon initially had fewer than two hundred employees worldwide, a far cry from the thousands at Four-Phase and Motorola. And Phil didn't windsurf, own an estate with a private lake, had no garage or even a car. And it didn't appear that any Enablon commemorative books were forthcoming for autograph sessions. Still, how could I ever forget the time he interrupted a meeting to welcome my son or the time he told me about the ditch swimming with chewy eyeballs, or the time he proudly paraded around in office in the black sports cap I had given him? And, after all, of the small number of CEOs I have known, Phil is the only one who actually interviewed and hired me.

Takeaway:
What makes leaders truly great (and successful) is the regard and appreciation they show toward those they are leading.

CHAPTER FIVE

ENABLON PASSION

Enablon started as a consulting software company. Armed with Marc's application server software, the two brothers, Dan and Marc, and their friend, Phil, initially asked clients what *they* wanted to do and constructed custom applications atop the server to meet client needs. So, at first, every client had a unique Enablon solution. This approach presents many challenges:

- Clients don't always know what they want, and the path to satisfying their wishes is often filled with plenty of detours and dead-ends. Enablon often saw the wisdom in the Steve Jobs quote: "People don't know what they want until you show it to them." And sometimes when clients do tell you what they want, you want to quote George W. Bush, who said, after hearing Donald Trump's inauguration speech, "That was some weird shit."
- It takes a lot of time. Enablon had to keep delving deeper, asking questions, clarifying what the client meant, and refining the software accordingly and continually. This sometimes seemed like a never-ending process. As Sidney Markowitz once said, "The software isn't finished until the last user is dead."
- It's hard to show off a lot of the work. Because the software was customized for every client, they had licensed it and typically objected to us showing their custom pieces to other potential Enablon clients (who could have potentially been their competitors).

Having such open-ended software can also create challenges when it comes to sales demos. A potential client provides a very sketchy set of requirements, allows no time to answer questions to clarify those requirements, and, midway through the demo, says, "No, that's not what I wanted at all." At times like these, validation (are we building the right software?) is more difficult than verification (are we building the software right?)

A classic story (passed down word-of-mouth from Enablonian to Enablonian—which may seem exaggerated and bordering on urban legend—but which I know is true because both Phil and Manny confirmed it) concerned an Enablon sales demo where the prospective clients provided very vague requirements and ended the initial demo shortly after it started. "Not at all what we wanted," they said. "No use going any farther, wasting our time and yours."

Phil was there. He quickly got them to, as he would say, "precise" what they wanted, then said, "Give us an hour and let us come back for a second chance."

The client reluctantly agreed.

Emmanuel (whose name salesman Ron always Americanized to "Manny") had joined Enablon by then and, software wizard that he was, was asked to totally reconfigure our software to meet the refined requirements. The client venue was busy and noisy, and poor Manny had nowhere quiet to concentrate except in a nearby restroom, where he set up shop in an unoccupied stall and went to work.

He delivered the revised demo on time. The client loved it, and in a flash (or should I say flush) signed a licensing agreement.

From this initiation into consulting, Enablon established some solid beliefs. These have become our culture, our passion, our reason for working tirelessly each day and for laying it on really thick in sentences like this:

- Provide intuitive baseline applications that clients can then easily tailor to their needs. Our initial "clean slate" approach often confounded clients with "choice overload."
- Focus these applications on improving the human condition by fostering a safer workplace and a cleaner environment. Our first application was Metrics, which allowed clients to better monitor the safety of their employees and the impact of their business on the environment, so they could take actions to mitigate potential and real hazards.
- Create and promote an atmosphere of "Yes, and..." in both our employees and our customers. As opposed

to our competitors, in Phil's words, "We would be agile where they were rigid, nimble where they were cumbersome, beautiful and modern where they looked old and dated, friendly and fun where they would be arrogant and stiff."

- Avoid working in restroom stalls, if at all possible.

I began to learn, even in my early days with Enablon, that when all these points (well, maybe not the last one) are in sync and work together in an organization, they bolster the morale and loyalty of both employees and customers.

A friend of mine at Motorola told me this story about a friend of his who was on his honeymoon at a swanky resort hotel. These friend-of-a-friend stories, I realize, get more and more exaggerated at each retelling, but, as apocryphal as it may be, it's a fabulous story—so what the hell. As the newlyweds were in the lobby, the husband spotted none other than...Michael Jordan, regarded by many (including most Chicagoans, that husband, and me) as the greatest basketball player who ever played the game. "It's Michael Jordan!" the newlywed exclaimed to his bride. "Michael Jordan—oh my gosh! MJ! Michael Jordan is right here!"

The man was being very loud and that perturbed Michael, who came closer to him and said, "Shush! Will you be quiet! I'm trying to enjoy my vacation—incognito—and you're drawing attention to me." This seemed ironic because Michael's six-foot, six-inch stature with a face recognized around the world would hardly go unnoticed, with or without some guy yelling his name. Michael apparently realized the irony too. When the husband apologized and looked down dejectedly, Michael asked him, "Do you play golf?"

"Of course, I love the game."

"I was just about to shoot a round. Care to join me?"

Imagine this opportunity. This newly-married man had an opportunity to play golf with one of his all-time sports idols. Wow! The man looked at Michael, then looked at his new bride, then back at Michael and back at his bride, and finally said, "No, I'm sorry. I just got married, and I think I should spend this time with my wife."

And *this* is the kind of loyalty that the Enablon key beliefs instill in both our employees and our customers. Other competitors may try to lure our employees or customers away from the Enablon camp, but like the newlywed, they respond, "No, I'm sorry." Granted, some may try to sneak away for a quick nine holes, but our key beliefs and culture continue to tug at them. Ours is a force that most cannot resist.

Takeaway:
The loyalty of both customers and employees is fostered by the nurturing, listening, and caring culture of a company.

I found our baseline applications extremely easy to learn. As I acquainted myself in Paris with the fine points of our Metrics application, I quickly grew confident that I could successfully deliver my first training session to our client in Denver soon after my return. And, should the client decide to change application features going forward, I found that easy to do as well.

As I worked more and more with Enablon software in Paris, I found it increasingly fun, and even addictive. A customer once asked me whether Enablon uses gamification techniques in its software. According to Merriam-Webster, gamification is "the process of adding games or gamelike elements to something (such as a task) so as to encourage participation."

Though I never saw any indication that Enablon was trying to produce its own version of M&Ms Eye Spy Pretzel game, the elements of gamification definitely exist in our software, should you wish to use them, like scoring, comparison of progress to other users, and rewards. This, together with the ability to easily build my own software elements or change those that already exist, made me want to spend more time "playing" with the software. It truly was becoming more of a pastime for me than a job. The terms "binge watching" and "binge gaming" hadn't even entered the mainstream in 2009, yet I was already binging on Enablon.

Not only did I find the Enablon software bingeable, I also began to appreciate how it helped the human condition. Increasingly, I saw examples of how clients were using our software to evaluate employee safety and environmental impact and implement action plans to address any shortcomings they found. Prior to working for Enablon, I had thought EHS could only mean Edwardsville High School, home of the Tigers in Edwardsville, Illinois. But now EHS—Environmental Health and Safety—took on a whole new meaning and, like the Enablon software itself, became an obsession with me. And I saw this in our clients and in my Enablon co-workers as well—a deep passion and commitment to make everyone's life safer and to protect our fragile planet Earth.

Margaret Mead once said, "Never doubt that a small group of thoughtful, committed, citizens can change the world. Indeed, it is the only thing that ever has." I was beginning to feel part (though an obviously weak member) of such a group—Enablon.

CHAPTER SIX

MOTIVATION

Dan Pink is one of my favorite authors. I had the honor to meet him at a talk he gave at a local university several years ago. In fact, I had even brought a book for him to sign, then realized I had picked up the wrong title (it was written by Malcolm Gladwell), so decided to forego the autograph scene, not wanting to duplicate the experience I had with Dennis Ritchie, described earlier.

In his book *Drive: The Surprising Truth About What Motivates Us*, Pink notes that there are three things that get us moving. Surprisingly, money is not one of them.

Now don't get me wrong. I am very much concerned about money. I can, at times, relate to the movie character Jerry Maguire, who ran around yelling, "Show me the money!" I recall during a very brief stint at the now long defunct Digital Equipment Corporation (DEC) being called into a meeting with a bunch of other employees to hear our manager announce our miniscule pay raise. He concluded by saying, "After all, we're not in this for the money."

To which I replied, "Ah, excuse me, you might not be in this for the money, but I think all the rest of us are. DEC is not a nonprofit organization, and we are not volunteers." My comment was met with applause from my co-workers. I quit DEC shortly thereafter. But the money really isn't the issue; it's the amount of money. As long as folks feel they are being paid a living wage (questionable, at least for me, at DEC) or are paying a reasonable amount for goods and services, money has little impact on their motivation and decisions.

There were times during the Motorola boom years that we got extremely generous bonuses, above and beyond our more-than-adequate salaries. I often had a hard time with that. Not hard enough to turn down the money. But, typically, I saw no connection with how hard I worked and the amount of my bonus, which was, after all, tied to company profitability. Some years I worked extremely hard, but our sales were soft and that meant less bonus. Other years I enjoyed more downtime, yet sales were hot, and the money rolled in. It wasn't the bonus money that motivated me. It was, rather, as Pink points out, three key factors that spark our enthusiasm:

1. Autonomy—the ability to be self-directed.
2. Mastery—available resources to learn what we need to know to succeed.
3. Passion—the ability to see our activities as contributing somehow to the greater good of all.

It occurred to me that Enablon hit the mark on all three. The software is easy to learn (and master) and use, thus making users more independent (and autonomous) in tailoring applications to their needs, contributing to the noble cause (and passion) of human safety and environmental protection. Does it sound like I am trying to sell you on Enablon? I will only say that I am also inspired by one of Pink's other books, *To Sell is Human.*

Motorola, like Enablon, excelled in those three areas while I was there. Motorolans, at least the ones I knew (as well as myself), were given much autonomy. In fact, the best-selling, groundbreaking RAZR phone (the phone that everyone just had to have in 2004) was developed in a Skunk Works by a small team of highly self-motivated engineers.

Many Motorolans were especially sensitive when it came to autonomy. I remember working with a fellow engineer during the afternoon of the day before a holiday. Our manager walked by and said, "You guys can go home now if you want." That manager thought he was being altruistic, but, after he left, my co-worker exploded in anger. "What a condescending twit! Our work time isn't something for him to give. If we're involved in a project and want to work, we work." And so we continued our work through the afternoon. I thought the anger was a bit over-reactive. After all, our manager had ended his sentence with "...if you want." We didn't want.

Motorola was noted for providing opportunities for mastery, as it produced one of the first corporate training centers—Motorola University (MU)—with a forty hour per year per employee training mandate from none other than Bob Galvin himself. MU even coordinated remote sessions with accredited universities, so employees could earn bona fide degrees. Such ongoing study is essential for high tech companies, according to Motorola statisticians who studied learning and told us that the half-life of technical training is four years (this was back in the early 2000s, it's probably much less now). That means that 50 percent of what a person learns is obsolete within four years.

For me, this was (at first) devastating news, because of what I was taught through my ongoing studies, I retained, at best, 5 percent. So every four years, only 2.5 percent of what I actually learned was still relevant. This did not make me feel very good about myself. I struggled to come to grips with this and eventually succeeded by convincing myself of the following:

- I was being extremely humble and retained much more than 5 percent.
- The half-life knowledge that I retained that was still relevant (however tiny that might be) was *very* relevant and key to the continued success of Motorola and all humankind.
- Regarding half-life statistics, I read somewhere and believed that 97.53 percent of all statistics are made

up. (Old joke, I know, but proven to get a laugh 84.37 percent of the time.)

Having opportunities to learn—not only in our area of specialty but above and beyond that—gives us the added confidence we need to step up when situations arise that stretch our abilities and enhance our job satisfaction. Award-winning record producer and acclaimed drummer Gregg Field, at a jazz seminar I attended many years ago, told an impressive story on the impact of mastery.

Gregg loved the artistry of Count Basie and his orchestra, so much so that he had memorized all their pieces. When they appeared locally, Gregg, a college student at the time, skipped his studies to attend each performance, before which he hung out at the back entrance of the theater to see if he could catch a glimpse of the orchestra and their phenomenal leader. One night, one of the band members singled out Gregg and said, "You've been here every night, haven't you?"

"Yes, I love listening to you guys." Gregg told the fellow about himself and how he played the drums.

"How would you like to meet Count Basie?"

"I'd be thrilled."

When Basie's limo pulled up, the band member escorted Gregg over to meet Basie. The introductions had just started when news arrived that Basie's regular drummer was ill and would not be able to perform.

"You say you play drums?" Basie asked Gregg, who, of course, said "yes."

"Maybe you can play with us tonight, eh?"

Gregg went through some practice pieces, did well, and was invited to stay. As the opening piece began, Gregg searched for the music. "Ah," one of the band members explained, "Our drummer doesn't use any music." But Gregg was prepared. He had practiced these Basie pieces so many times that they were etched in his brain. He fit right in.

He was later asked to join the Basie orchestra full-time in the 1980s and went on to enjoy a distinguished career as musician, arranger, record producer, and music educator. All because he was prepared. This is mastery. But let's not forgot autonomy, too. Gregg took his own initiative to break away from the routine of his college studies to absorb real-life performance. And, finally, let's not forget passion. Gregg's mastery of Basie's music would never have been possible without the passion he felt for that magnificent Basie sound and the great feeling and satisfaction it brings—like all great music—to listeners everywhere.

Similarly, there was a Motorola passion. Not to play drums with Count Basie (as honorable as that might be), but something broader. A compelling overall desire and impulse to strive toward some noble cause embedded in the corporate DNA—to promote and support public safety. In 1930, Motorola first sold car radio-receivers (high tech back then) to police and local governments. The company, over its long life, embarked on many businesses including car radios, semi-conductors, auto components, televisions, computer systems, satellite networks, set-top boxes, barcode and RFID readers, pagers, and, of course, portable phones. Nevertheless, the DNA that emerged in 1930 had the strongest impact on the company. Motorola Solutions, all that remains of the original Motorola after it was divvied up and sold off in small chunks, is still focused, as of this writing, on improving public safety via high tech communications.

Ironically, Enablon's DNA involves safety as well, but from the perspective of improving employees' work environment and making our planet a healthier place. Wanting to "eat our own dog food," Enablon used its technology to create a system called "Enablon Office" or simply "EO," wherein we can log our project time, track resources, file expenses, and manage overall office operations. But the DNA is missing. The passion isn't there. Enablon Office doesn't make life safer or less risky for employees or protect the environment. As far as I know, we've never sold it to anyone outside Enablon, nor have we ever tried. The spark to improve it and make it shine just isn't there. I have heard some employees say, "EO is BO." I like to think of it as an old, sometimes clunky, sometimes dated—but still very useful—artifact, kind of the way I like to think of myself.

Amazon's Jeff Bezos nailed it when he said, "I strongly believe that missionaries make better products. They care more. For a missionary, it's not just about the business. There has to be a business, and the business has to make sense, but that's not why you do it. You do it because you have something meaningful that motivates you." It is that missionary-like passion that is a major factor in employee enthusiasm.

Along those same lines, the ever-enthusiastic Teddy Roosevelt once said, "Nobody cares how much you know until they know how much you care." In my role, I began to see that simply managing knowledge wasn't enough at Enablon, but that knowledge had to be supported by caring—caring about employees and customers, caring about their safety, caring about our environment. Yes, and also caring about "Yes, and...."

Takeaway:
Success is fed by autonomy, a thirst for learning, and missionary-like passion.

Yes, And...

What reinforces autonomy, mastery, and passion for both employees and clients is a pervasive "Yes, and..." attitude. Without it, none of these three motivators would even be possible. The "Yes, and..." approach is a vital component of improvisation. Tina Fey mentioned it in her hilarious book *Bossypants*. Improv is such a vital component that we had two Enablon-sponsored workshops in it (with heavy emphasis on "Yes, and...") taught by a Chicago Second City improv instructor and friend of Tina. And, my good friend Pamela Meyer, in her thought-provoking business book, *The Agility Shift*, writes, "The core principle of improvisation is to say, 'Yes, and...' while supporting the scene with further detail. Successful improvisors accept whatever they are given, no matter how outlandish, and build on that scenario with delight and curiosity."

Let's take the opening of an improv skit and consider it from three perspectives.

Opening #1.

Actor A: Wow, I love eating at this restaurant, don't you? The fish here are especially tasty!

Actor B: And I am driving my red sports car down Route 66.

This is not "Yes, and..." This is "No." Actor B did not add anything to what Actor A had offered. B, in effect, told A, "No, I don't want this sketch to be about restaurants or fish or what you consider tasty. I am completely changing the story to be about my red sports car and Route 66." The kiss of death for successful improvisation.

Opening #2.

Actor A: Wow, I love eating at this restaurant, don't you? The fish here are especially tasty!

Actor B: Speaking of fish, I have a pet goldfish. His name is Twinkles.

This is also not "Yes, and..." This is "Yes, but..." Actor B acknowledged Actor A's mention of fish and essentially said, "Yes, let's continue this sketch about fish, BUT not in the context of a restaurant or what you think is tasty. Let's shift it to my pet goldfish." Another kiss of death.

In some ways, "Yes, but..." is worse than "No." "No" at least is honest and straightforward. "Yes, but..." tries, in a sneaky way, to make the target think there is agreement and enhancement, but then includes changes to negate the original flow. It tends to be the most popular (and weasel-like) way to say "No."

Opening #3

Actor A: Wow, I love eating at this restaurant, don't you? The fish here are especially tasty!

Actor B: Oh, you are so right! I absolutely devour the breaded European eel they serve here, though I think it's on the top ten endangered fish species list. The place would probably get shut down if the authorities found out. But I'm not talking. What's your favorite?

Finally, "Yes, and...." Actor B embellished what Actor A said while retaining A's focus on restaurant, fish, and taste, then threw it back to A for more.

Employees can't thrive when the desire for autonomy, mastery, and passion that they bring to their work is met by their company with, "Yes, but..." or when customers eagerly seek products and services and face the response, "Yes, but...."

I learned very early that Enablon fostered "Yes, and..." ("*Oui et*" in French). When new ideas and suggestions sprang from employees or customers, the response invariably was "Yes, and we can...." No doubt, this positive culture emerged from Enablon's early beginnings of pure consulting, where essentially the "product" was whatever the client wanted it to be. Even though Enablon reduced the open-endedness of its offerings (to reduce the anxiety of a total "clean slate" approach), that willingness to listen and act very much remained.

When "Yes, and..." is missing, the results are disastrous. To illustrate, I present an experience I had in early 2018 at a large popular nationwide retail store whose name ends with a "t" (at least you know it's not Costco). I keep the name nearly anonymous for four reasons:

1. The reader may work for this store or have friends and relatives who work for the store and I don't want you to hate me.
2. I sincerely hope the store has changed since my experience, and, if so, hurray! I don't want to continue giving the store (that has hopefully changed its ways) horrible publicity in this book.
3. The store may be a current or potential Enablon customer and I certainly don't want to irk them.
4. I thought the reader might have fun trying to guess the company. If you have been to any of their stores, maybe you know instantly which retailer I am talking about, but I'll never tell.

I will henceforth refer to the store as ***t.

My wife Chris is not a heavy smartphone user. She had been using a rather dated Tracfone. My son Doug had traded in his smartphone for the latest model and suggested that my wife switch to his old phone (which was still much newer than hers). His old phone could still be functional on the Tracfone network if his current SIM (subscriber identify module) card was replaced with a Tracfone SIM card. So, all we had to do was buy the Tracfone SIM card, make the switch, and coordinate with Tracfone to activate the phone on their network.

We searched online for the SIM card we needed and found it at a variety of websites, including Amazon (of course), as well as ***t. The cost of the card was a remarkably cheap ninety-nine cents. As luck (or maybe misfortune) would have it, Doug and I happened to be driving around on Friday before we made any online purchase and happened to pass a ***t. "Hey," Doug suggested, "since we're right here, why don't we go in and buy the SIM card for mom now? Then we can activate her phone as soon as we get home."

That sounded good to me.

We entered ***t, went directly to the electronics section, and found the Tracfone SIM card—only it was marked $9.99. Thinking it was a mistake, we found the ***t associate in electronics and asked him to do a price check. "No," he said, after doing the check. "The price is correct. It is $9.99."

"Your own website is selling it for ninety-nine cents," I said. "Can't you honor that price?" My son showed him the ***t site on his smartphone.

"*Yes, but* I can only do price matching up to ten percent."

"But you are price matching against your own store."

"*Yes, but* that is our policy."

Now I had already received two "*Yes, buts*" from the ***t associate, so at this point, I pulled out a piece of scrap paper and began tabulating them. The associate looked at me curiously, no doubt wondering what I was scribbling.

"So," I persisted, "it seems that ***t is selling a product at two different prices. That doesn't seem right, does it?"

"*Yes, but* we aren't told the prices of the online items—so there's no way for us to know. They have their online prices and we have ours."

Now we could have just shrugged and left at this point, but I was having too much fun. "I'd like to talk to a manager."

"Sure." The electronics associate replied very calmly and matter-of-factly, as though his being asked to fetch a manager was a very common occurrence. He led us to the front of the store, spoke privately at first to one manager, who then motioned to another, then another, and finally there were four ***t managers at the front of the store discussing our ninety-nine cent SIM card.

"Okay," one of them finally told us. "You can buy the SIM card for ninety-nine cents."

"Super. I knew you would honor your online price."

"*Yes, but* you'll have to buy it online."

"But we're already at the front of the store and the check-out register is right here."

"*Yes, but* since the price was listed online, you'll have to purchase it online. Then you'll have the SIM card—no problem."

Fine. Doug purchased the ninety-nine-cent SIM card online via his smartphone. We showed the purchase confirmation to the managers and were ready to take the SIM card home. "Okay?"

"*Yes, but* you'll have to first go to the back of the store to our pick-up area. They'll confirm your purchase, then you can go."

With the SIM card in my hand, we walked to the back of the store to the pick-up department and described the situation to the department associate. "Okay," I concluded. "Purchase confirmed. Can we go?"

"*Yes, but* you can't take that SIM card. Since you purchased it online, it must come from our online inventory. It's not in stock right now, but you should be able to pick it up on Monday."

"But it is in my hand. I paid for it. Why can't I just take it and go? I don't want to drive all the way back here on Monday for something I have right now. If I ordered this on Amazon, for the same price, I could have it delivered to my door by tomorrow. Why should I wait until Monday and then have to drive all the way back here to get it?"

He looked at me straight in the eyes and nodded knowingly with a slight smile, as if to say, "I hear you. I buy all my stuff from Amazon too."

"Can I see your manager?"

"Sure."

"Can't we just take this SIM card?" I asked the pick-up manager. "It's already been paid for online. Your co-worker can confirm that."

"*Yes, but* it's an online purchase. Has to come from that inventory."

"Okay, then. I don't want the SIM card. I'll buy it on Amazon." As I said this, I couldn't help but notice the associate giving me another knowing smile. It took the pick-up manager at least ten minutes to figure out how to negate our online ninety-nine-cent purchase. He punched keys on his register, asked for Doug's smartphone so he could copy numbers from the online sales confirmation, then he punched more register keys, then asked for Doug's smartphone again to copy more numbers, then more typing, until the deed was done. We couldn't even get the departing satisfaction of a hot dog and soft drink for $1.50—no "t" at the end of Costco.

Eight "Yes, buts" and forty-five minutes later, seven ***t associates had failed to sell a ninety-nine-cent item (actually $1.09 with tax) and, worse, created without any apologies a potentially disgruntled customer. I wasn't really disgruntled, though I think I had every right to be. I found the whole situation quite amusing, and sad.

Vital ingredients to retail (and really all sales endeavors) are:

- To sell product.
- To make customers happy so they return.

Employees at ***t lacked the passion and the training and the autonomy to provide those ingredients. I don't blame the employees. To me, they were as victimized as the customers by a company culture devoid of people-focus. The heads of

***t obviously hadn't read Dan Pink, or studied improvisation, or tried to buy a ninety-nine-cent SIM card at one of their retail stores.

A friend of mine told me a "Yes, and..." success story. It is the antithesis of my ***t experience.

As an out-of-town visitor, my friend had dinner at a local seafood restaurant. When his waiter, Jimmy, asked what he would care to drink, my friend replied, "Pepsi, please."

"We have Coke. Is that okay?"

"I really prefer Pepsi."

This could have been a "Yes, but..." moment for Jimmy, who could have responded, "Yes, but Coke is all we have." Instead he held his tongue. He was thinking "Yes, and...."

"I guess," my friend continued, "Coke will have to do."

A few moments later, Jimmy, a bit out of breath, returned with a bottle of Pepsi.

"I thought you said you only had Coke."

"We do," said Jimmy. "But you said you prefer Pepsi, so I hurried over to the corner convenience store, bought some Pepsi, and brought it back for you."

"You paid for it out of your own pocket?"

“I figured the generous tip you will leave will more than make up for the price of the Pepsi.”

My friend smiled. He had just been “Yes, anded.” Every time he visited from out of town, he ate at that seafood restaurant. They did not serve breaded European eel (on the top ten endangered fish species list, you may recall) so there was no danger of the place being shut down. He and Jimmy became good friends. Then one day, Jimmy was gone. No longer there to wait on him. “What happened to Jimmy?” my friend asked the new waiter.

“Oh, he got promoted. He’s now the manager of this place.”

I must admit that after my initial interview with Phil, which was chock-full of “Yes, buts,” I had thought the Enablon culture might be like that previously described at ***t.

But the customer case studies I examined as I learned about Enablon during my two-week initiation in Paris convinced me of the opposite. A client had a desire (like my desire to pay the online price of ninety-nine cents), presented it to an Enablon representative (no need to seek a higher-up manager to get attention), and there was follow-up (“Yes, and....”). Most of our software products, in fact, have evolved this way – from client and employee suggestions/requests that have been met with "Yes, and..." Enablon is a company of Jimmys.

Takeaway:
Yes, be a "Yes, and..." person, and grow and nurture the ideas and notions of those around you.

CHAPTER SEVEN

BUT BACK TO PARIS

My two weeks in Paris flew by. I had spent Halloween 2009 there and was shocked that nobody dressed up or went trick-or-treating or hung out jack-o'-lanterns. I had brought a clown costume along in anticipation, but when I observed no one else in costume, I decided not to wear it (though I did put on the red nose—just briefly).

When it finally came time for me to leave, I didn't realize that I would only visit the Enablon office at Boulevard Georges Clemenceau one more time in my life (Enablon

Paris would eventually relocate to a brand-new nearby office complex). My return would come almost two years later, for meetings with Angela and our KM Paris team. It would be much less jam-packed than my first visit, but it would also start out with the most bizarre twist I have ever experienced.

For my second visit to the Paris office, I decided to bring my whole family—my wife Chris and our three teenage children. I also had a debit card this time. No more masquerading as Mr. Bartholome, the coffee table book author.

I would spend the first week working while my family went sightseeing, then take off the second week to join the family vacation. By then, Enablon Chicago had hired an associate to support office operations and travel. Browsing the internet, she had found a most economical deal for accommodations for my second Paris visit, even better than Hotel Hermes. She reserved the accommodations online with a contact named Rodrigo. Rodrigo sent me an email a week prior to our departure. "Got down payment wire transfer. Kindly wait further details on rooms." I was suspicious of Rodrigo for several reasons:

- His name seemed phony to me. It didn't match his email address, which was a jumble of letters followed by @yahoo.fr. And I had never known a Rodrigo before, only the one in Shakespeare's Othello, and he had not been one of the great bard's most endearing characters.

- Nowhere in his email did Rodrigo provide any other contact information, like his full name, company, postal address, or phone number.
- His email was so short. No "Dear..., Thank you for...." Even a "Yes, but..." would have been appreciated.

Despite my misgivings, I waited eagerly for Rodrigo and hoped I was wrong. We were leaving on Sunday and it was Friday. Still no "further details" from Rodrigo. Our travel associate tried to contact him during the week. No response. She was frantically looking into alternatives, thinking that she had been duped and that the Enablon wire transfer to this bogus hotel rep was money lost. On Saturday, I was really getting nervous. Then that afternoon, an email from Rodrigo, albeit a very brief one. "Rooms arranged." This was followed by *two* Paris addresses.

"Please clarify," I emailed back. "Which is the correct address?"

His reply email came surprisingly fast. "Sorry. The first." I was relieved. I phoned our travel associate, told her Rodrigo had come through, and that she no longer had to worry that she had been scammed. This, after all, was a budget operation, and I perhaps was expecting too much from poor Rodrigo. I had my address. I was happy.

We arrived in Paris early Monday morning and took a taxi to the address Rodrigo had indicated. Our driver spoke little English but understood the address I had printed.

It was the address of a restaurant.

"Must be upstairs," I told Chris and the kids as I went inside to explore, while they stayed in the taxi. I asked the restaurant staff to direct me to the guest rooms. The staff didn't understand much English either, but I could see that the upstairs had more restaurant tables and chairs. There were no guest rooms. This was not a hotel or apartment complex. Rodrigo had deceived us. Our travel associate *had* been ripped off and Enablon was out the money that had been wire transferred.

There we were. The Barr family, somewhere in Paris after an eight-hour airplane flight, with no place to stay, in a taxi full of luggage, with a driver who could not understand us, and without a cell phone that worked in France. None of us spoke French. I had learned nothing of the language after two years—despite what I had originally told Phil, shame on me. I certainly hadn't managed my own knowledge of French very well, had I?

I had one of Angela's business cards with the Enablon Paris office address at Boulevard Georges Clemenceau and showed that to the driver, who understood and drove us to Enablon. We five Barrs—with all our luggage—piled into the front reception area of Enablon Paris. Angela immediately greeted us, and I explained the situation. In her sweet and diplomatic way, she indicated that she just didn't believe me. She knew I was direction-challenged and spoke no French, so I figured she thought I had taken my family to the wrong address and/or didn't understand what the people at that address were telling me. She was certainly half-right; I didn't understand the folks at the restaurant one bit.

She acted quickly and decisively, with a people-focus and charm so representative of Enablon. First, she knew my wife and kids looked dead tired, so she arranged for them to be taken to a local hotel temporarily to rest until the Rodrigo issue was settled. I emphasize "temporarily" here because this available local hotel was quite expensive, and I really didn't want to stay there during week two, when I was completely footing the bill for our vacation. With my family packed into a taxi and on their way, she turned to me and said, "Come."

We got into another cab and headed for the address Rodrigo had given us. I didn't know how to say "I told you so" in French, otherwise I think I would have blurted it out. Sure enough, it was a restaurant. Angela spoke quickly in French to some of the restaurant staff, then shook her head. "You said this Rodrigo fellow gave you a second address?"

I showed it to her. It was within walking distance, she said, so we headed there on foot. We arrived to find a small dress shop. Angela shook her head again, then went inside. I followed and heard her immediately speaking in French to the female proprietor of the place.

They spoke for a very long time and I couldn't understand a word, except for an occasional "*Qui.*" At first, I thought that maybe Angela was in the process of purchasing a new dress. Finally, Angela turned to me with a weak smile and said, "This girl" (Angela called all females "girls") "says her cousin has a flat he is trying to rent and might be willing to rent it to you for two weeks. She's going to call him."

I was suspicious. What a coincidence! Who was this cousin? I wondered whether it was the infamous Rodrigo.

As it turns out, the cousin was willing to rent the flat (which turned out to be fantastic, including a balcony with a wonderful view of idyllic French street cafes below) for a very reasonable rate. However, I insisted that payment for the flat be made *at the end* of each week's stay *in cash*. No more shady prepayment shenanigans. The cousin agreed, and my family and I could not have asked for better accommodations. However, we never did see this mysterious cousin. His sister (or so she said) came to pick up the rent after each of our two weeks. Was this cousin really Rodrigo? Did he want to avoid us for fear that he might slip up and divulge his true identify? Was that why the rent on the apartment was so reasonable, because he had already ripped off Enablon for a substantial down payment? I will never know, but out of my unending curiosity I have sent Rodrigo several emails since. He has never replied.

The apartment we were renting was in a marvelous central location in Paris, and, though it was extremely convenient the first week for my family's sightseeing, it meant I had to take the train to work. No easy walk from the Hotel Hermes this time. Angela had carefully mapped out which train I should take, where I would catch that train, and where I would walk once I got off the train. With my terrible sense of direction, I still managed to get lost several times but somehow always recovered and found my way.

One day I had a leisurely lunch with two Enablon sales reps, Ian and Steven. Ian shared his dour interviewing experience with Phil, who had stared into his laptop the whole time and then had finally declared, non-enthusiastically, "Okay, let's give this a try."

Both Ian and Steven were from England originally but now lived in France and could speak French. I love sales people as, from my experiences, they always seem upbeat and energetic, and I now related to these two as well because while they sold Enablon products, I sold Enablon knowledge. It was a delightful lunch and an especially lucky one for me, as events the next day would prove.

That next morning, I was proud of myself as I walked directly to the train station without a single wrong turn. The train came promptly, as it had on previous days, and I sat down, listening eagerly for when my stop would be called, "*Courbevoie*" (pronounced "Cor-bev-wah").

The train stopped at the next station (not *Courbevoie*), an announcement in French came over the loudspeaker, and all the people on the train started to get off. I didn't know what to do. I decided to follow the crowd and get off, and the empty train pulled out of the station.

A few minutes later, another train arrived. Everyone got back on. I did too. Two more stations, and another announcement in French, but now some people got off and some people stayed on. What to do now? I asked some people around me what was happening, but they didn't speak English. I was frozen. The train doors were about to close. Should I stay, and, if I did, would this train take me to *Courbevoie* and Enablon or someplace unknown? I was truly panicked. And then I saw him...Steven. He was on the train too and grabbed my arm and pulled me off the train with him.

"Am I glad to see you, Steven! What's happening?"

"There's a strike of the railway engineers. The train we were on was going to be delayed by forty-five minutes to an hour. You certainly don't want to sit there. We're at the station just before *Courbevoie,* only about a five-minute walk to the Enablon office. Hope you don't mind a short stroll."

"Not a bit."

As I reflect on these two adventures in Paris during my second visit, I can't help but make analogies to Enablon. There I was (like a typical customer), having carefully planned what I wanted to do (as with my family's living accommodations or my train ride), when the provider of the services I counted on (like Rodrigo or the French rail system) failed me and I was lost, but then came Enablon (in the form of Angela or Steven), which guided me to success. Okay, maybe you don't like my analogy, but as Sigmund Freud once said, "Analogies, it is true, decide nothing, but they can make one feel more at home." And every year, I saw myself and my clients feel more at home with Enablon. Okay, maybe you don't like Sigmund Freud either.

Takeaway:
Be proud of your company. Promote it whenever possible. Readily analogize it to an important helper or guide. If you lack the passion to do this, you are in the wrong job.

CHAPTER EIGHT

BACK HOME

Returning to the US after my initial two-week training stay in Paris, I attacked my work full-force. The Denver onsite training, held one week after I returned, went surprisingly well. Its success, I think, can be attributed to four factors:

1. The client participants in the training were extremely kind and very new to our software.

2. The software system the client had licensed was very simple and straightforward without any unusual configuration or customization.
3. I had added confidence in my delivery because Enablon had sent Arnaud with me to have my back if I screwed up and to give me moral support.
4. I wore my lucky socks.

My luck continued—even without Arnaud or the socks—as I delivered many more training sessions in both the US and Canada that people seemed to enjoy. At least, no one exhibited any hostile behavior: no screams, obscenities, threats, name-calling, or other belligerent manifestations. Success.

Along the way, I came to know and befriend many of my colleagues at Enablon North America Corporation. Two of these were sales reps: Ron, whom I mentioned earlier, the American who moved to Paris then returned to America as part of Phil's expedition in 2008, and John, a burly Texan originally from Louisiana, one of the first American locals hired by Enablon. Both Ron and John worked in a makeshift office in Houston in hopes of landing many deals in the lucrative oil and gas industry. They frequently visited our Willis Tower office in Chicago, and they added a spark whenever they appeared. Ron would visit everyone in the office, effortlessly navigating from English to French. For any sales deal, regardless of how remote it might seem to achieve, he would boom, "We can do this *indeed*!" Indeed, "Indeed" became a popular slogan in the office.

John somehow seemed to take a liking to me and at times has called me "Big Daddy" and "*The Greatest* of All Time." Indeed. Of course, I, Big Daddy, sometimes wondered, "The Greatest *what* of All Time?"

One time, Ron and John decided to have me visit them in Houston for a sales meeting. I usually didn't do sales meetings, but the potential client was asking a lot of questions about training, so Ron and John figured it might be best to have me there to provide details.

When I arrived at their small Houston office in my customary client-interfacing suit and tie, they had ordered lunch, and I joined them. Ron was wearing a flamboyant white puffy shirt, a subdued version of the one Seinfeld wore in the episode appropriately entitled "The Puffy Shirt." John, also in suit and tie, had an obvious food stain on the front of his shirt that Ron pointed out, raising his puffy sleeves.

Midway through lunch, Ron's phone rang. He scooted off to answer it, then returned exclaiming, "Oh, shoot. The times are mixed up. They expect to meet with us an hour earlier. One-thirty, not two-thirty." It was almost one-fifteen. "We've got to go."

We hurried out to the cars. I rode with John. Ron drove separately. I noticed that Ron had a clothing bag in the back of his car. I assumed they would change once we got to the client site.

"No, problem," John assured me, as we pulled out of the parking lot. "We'll still get there on time. It's just down the road."

"Just down the road" in Texas terms means about twenty-five miles minimum. We seemed to be driving forever, and arrived slightly late, but joined the potential clients in their large meeting room. Ron still sported the puffy shirt, and John had retained his stain. But that didn't matter. Ron and John didn't focus on themselves. Their razor-sharp concentration could not be distracted by ornate shirts or food stains. What mattered supreme to these two was the prospective client. The sincerity, friendliness, empathy, and persistence of these two guys eventually closed the deal. Indeed.

Their secret, and that of all Enablon sales reps and of all Enablonians whom I have observed, is simple: Listen to the client or potential client and get them involved. To paraphrase a popular quote: "Those who don't listen will eventually be surrounded by people who have nothing to say." The client has *plenty* to say, to help you make a sale and to help you improve your product, but they won't tell you much if they don't think you are listening to them. Ron and John are good talkers but, through all their pleasantries, it is also clear that they are listening, intensely. Except, of course, for the time of the Houston client meeting I attended with them, which was one-thirty, not two-thirty.

The same approach, I have seen, is equally important in knowledge management, where I am selling not product, but knowledge. Clients tell me the best way to teach them, but I must listen and get them involved.

Takeaway:
Listen to your clients, engage them, partner with them, get them involved.

CHAPTER NINE

LESSONS LEARNED

Knowledge management is not about me. It is about my clients and co-workers. This point hit me squarely in the head during my first Enablon internal seminar.

Enablon internal seminars, held annually—usually in January—became a part of Enablon North America tradition, a time when management would communicate overall business plans for the year, where departments would report on past, present, and upcoming initiatives, and where Enablonians would come together in some fun team-building. As knowledge manager, I was asked to give a brief presentation to the team.

I remember walking up to the front of the group, the details of what I had planned to say running through my mind. I had been mapping out my presentation for several days. After all, this was my first internal seminar speech, and, after only a few months on the job, I wanted to impress. I would list all the things (real and imagined) that I had done, all the obstacles and challenges I had encountered, and all the many ways I had overcome potential problems to succeed (in my opinion).

I stood there, looking at our small team, ready to deliver my speech, and then, as I opened my mouth, immediately realized that what I had planned to say was bullshit. In a moment of pure improvisation, I started pointing out all those who had helped me. My presentation wasn't about me, it was about my co-workers. I thanked and praised them for all their help in my attempts to succeed as a knowledge manager. I had listened carefully to all their guidance and suggestions and now they were listening as I showed my appreciation. When I was finished, several of them came over to tell me, "Best speech of the seminar!" How can you not like a speech that calls you out by name and says you are great? Phil congratulated me too. I think he seemed to especially like my comment about his having the "coolest written signature"—which he really does.

I took this same approach to teaching in-person classes. Not praising participants' signatures but getting them involved. We all need each other, and the more we make learning experiences a partnership of all participants, not just a one-sided performance by the "teacher," the more successful those experiences become. I witnessed an obvious example of our need for others during a taxicab ride to the airport from a hotel in Mexico City, where I had been conducting a training session for a client.

The driver spoke no English but was given written instructions in Spanish to take me to the airport. He was a smiling, friendly fellow, but had no idea of how to get to the airport from the hotel. He had no smartphone or GPS and my smartphone was not functional in Mexico. Nevertheless, the driver was unphased. He would drive for a bit, seem lost (I know the feeling), then roll down the car window and yell at a passerby for directions, then drive on. Drive, stop, ask passersby, drive. This continued at least a half-dozen times until we reached the airport. The driver used the human GPS system, relying on others to guide him to his destination.

Isn't this what learning and knowledge management and companies like Enablon, and ultimately life, are all about? Sometimes we are the drivers, seeking help from those we meet along the way, and other times we are the passersby, supplying guidance to help others reach their goals. Of course, an actual GPS device is also helpful, especially if the weather is very hot and rolling down the taxi's window kills the air conditioning.

I recall one three-day training session I did for a client onsite where another Enablonian from our Paris office, Edouard, observed me. He had never done training before and was considering delivering some sessions in Europe to help Angela and the knowledge management team in Paris. "How do you measure the success of your training?" he asked me prior to the session.

"As the class goes on, I should do less and less. By the end of the session, I should be doing hardly anything. That is success."

He stared at me, quite puzzled. From the start of the class, I asked for volunteers, who worked on the Enablon software from my laptop, which was projected onto a screen for all participants to see. They also logged in to the software and worked along with the volunteer. I gave verbal directions on what to do.

As we progressed, I gave fewer and fewer directions and asked participants what we should do to successfully work with the software. By the end of the session, I was asking volunteers to provide on-the-job scenarios of how Enablon software could be used and to lead participants in what they should do to complete those scenarios. In effect, the clients were teaching themselves.

I glanced at Edouard and nodded. Success! How could the clients complain about the training session? They were running it. They were taking ownership of their own learning.

When this happens, sometimes I see students experience an "ah-ha" moment, when something they didn't quite understand suddenly makes sense, when they suddenly answer their own questions. The experience is much like that described in the story of the crayon art class.

The art student was having difficulty getting any color from his crayon. He kept rubbing the paper with it, but no color appeared. "I can't remember where I put my white crayon," the student declared, frustrated. "This crayon just isn't working. The white crayon is what I need. Where did I put that white crayon?"

His teacher made a brief observation. "That crayon isn't working because it is not a crayon."

"What is it?"

"It's a glycerin suppository."

"Ah-hah! Now I know where I put my white crayon!"

Some people regard a teacher as a "sage on the stage"—a person of extreme wisdom who stands before an audience to promulgate abundant information. I struggle with this approach because:

- I am not smart enough to be considered a sage.
- I cannot lecture to people for even short periods of time without boring them to death.
- Delivering a training session in-person is not a performance, like a theatrical stage, but rather a partnership with clients to empower them to learn.
- I prefer to be known as a "guide on the side" (or, as rephrased by some students, the "jerk who has us work").

Takeaway:
When tasked with helping people learn, be a "guide on the side," not a "sage on the stage."

Nevertheless, delivering training sessions is not always a happy experience. Though I certainly was swaggering after my demonstration for Edouard, I have had times when I wanted to crawl into a hole and die. During one large in-person class (over fifty people), I met with criticism from the group after every sentence I uttered.

I would point out one feature of the Enablon software.

The volunteer at my laptop, projecting to the screen, would painfully navigate to where I had directed her, emitting an agonized sigh.

One of the participants would shout out, "Yes, but we have been doing it another way..." and he would then explain the way he had been performing the process—either with paper and pencil or on very dated software no longer sold—for the past decade. Others in the class would provide exaggerated nods of agreement.

I would point out another feature.

My volunteer would again agonize.

Another "Yes, but..." and more nods of agreement.

After several more "Yes, buts," I smiled, called a break, and spoke to the group's manager, who had been sitting in the back of the room, looking pale. He had been part of the company's purchasing committee who had licensed the

Enablon software. "I think we need to backtrack," I suggested. "Perhaps if you first explained *how* the Enablon software saves folks time and makes their jobs easier, I won't run into so much resistance. Then folks will be more motivated to learn."

I didn't intimately know the employees' work processes and, even if I did, I wouldn't have the credibility of their manager. He heartily agreed and did a very effective job of stepping the training back and convincing participants of the benefits they would see from our software on the job. It took several hours of back-and-forth, but participants eventually saw the light and I followed-up with what turned out to be quite a successful session on how to use our tool. During the follow-up, the "Yes, buts..." were replaced with lots of "Yes, ands..." as participants not only appreciated the software's functionality but actively began to "and" how that functionality could be extended into work processes. And color had returned to their manager's face.

Takeaway:
People must understand and accept the advantages of a new tool or process before they feel motivated to learn it.

I never try to coerce a participant to volunteer to work from my laptop and project for all to see. But sometimes members of the class are voluntold by their manager to come up. Such was the case with a poor elderly (even older than me) woman whose boss thought it would be "a great learning opportunity" for her. The woman was not very computer savvy and extremely nervous in front of the group. In my most soothing and gentle voice, I directed her on how to proceed on my laptop. Her fingers trembled. She started Microsoft Word. Then Excel. A browser window was already open with our Enablon application ready to go. She closed the window. She wasn't listening to my soothing and gentle voice.

"Okay," I told her. "I'm glad you did that. These are common mistakes people make." Not common at all. "It's actually good when we make mistakes like these during training, so we'll remember them and won't make them on the job. So, thank you. And now let's step back a bit. Can you open your browser?" Slowly, I told her step-by-step what to do. She was finally in the Enablon software, but it took such a long time. Members of the class were strangely attentive, curious, I think, to see how long I could go on with this woman before having a meltdown. Her boss was covering his mouth, concealing a chuckle. I thought it was cruel to make fun of the poor woman. I have never ever in any way thought of poking fun at a client learning our software because:

- It goes completely counter to our Enablon culture (which I heartily embrace) that puts the customer first and in our highest regard. I have no aspirations to be the Don Rickles of knowledge management.
- Our clients are all much smarter than I am—they are EHS professionals, chemists, environmentalists, and experts in regulatory compliance and risk and change management. They may not know our software initially, but it usually doesn't take long for them to learn. I am simply an advisor who tries to point them in the right direction.
- I save up all my energy to poke fun at our competitors, like I*x, G*e, E*x, and others (fill in the * with one or more missing letters, though you can't fill in the missing functionality and usability).

After a few more instructions, my volunteer was becoming more confident. She was now navigating the software, at my direction, with apparent ease. No more trembling. Wow! I had asked the other participants to mimic her keystrokes on their laptops. "Does anyone remember how to access the reports?" I was staring directly at her boss, and he felt compelled to answer.

"I think—"

My volunteer lady cut him off, told me the right answer, and demonstrated it on my laptop for all to see. The boss had been right after all. Volunteering had proven "a great learning opportunity." And now she was the one who was chuckling.

Getting participants engaged promotes optimal learning but can be dangerous when participants don't agree with each other. On one memorable occasion, my volunteer was busy following my instructions. The class members were watching the projected screen and mirroring the volunteer's actions on their laptops, when suddenly several participants exclaimed, "This isn't right. Our process doesn't work this way. The system isn't configured correctly."

"It sure is," replied several others.

"No, whose idea was it that the software should work like this?"

"Our idea. We went through several configuration workshops, and this is what we decided."

"How come we weren't involved in those workshops? This set-up is wrong!"

Now one of the participants turned on me. "Why didn't you notice the problems with this set-up?"

"Because I am unfamiliar with the internal processes of your company."

"But you're the teacher. You should be familiar with the processes of all departments. How can you work for our company and not know the processes?"

"Because I don't work for your company. I work for Enablon, the vendor who provides this software."

"Oh...sorry."

"No problem. My fault, really. I should have made that clear at the beginning of the session." I had mentioned it several times. But I prefer to apologize for being unclear when clients say something silly, hoping they may return the favor when it's my turn.

The client factions resumed their internal battle. Back and forth the debate raged on. Rather than "guide on the side," I wanted to "hide on the side." No punches were thrown. Eventually, both sides agreed to have upper management intervene, and it was decided that our training session should morph into a requirements-gathering activity, where all participants could agree on how the system should be configured. There were lots of "Yes, ands..." during that session, as the group became engaged in how to expand expectations.

In my encounters with clients, Enablon has always provided an intuitive baseline of applications that clients can then easily tailor to their needs. However, sometimes, as in the volatile disagreement just described, clients come to a hasty decision on how to tailor our software without first getting feedback and consensus from all their key stakeholders. Lewis Carroll, obviously foreseeing the future of Enablon clients making impulsive configuration decisions, warned, "The hurrier I go, the behinder I get."

Takeaway:
A product or service cannot meet client expectations that were never clearly defined.

CHAPTER TEN

ALTERNATIVES AND CHALLENGES

"Do you always do the volunteer shtick for in-person training?" people ask me. No. Sometimes my audience is very small, so the session turns into an intimate interactive discussion group. Sometimes participants are in and out so much of the session that it is impossible to keep a volunteer for any reasonable length of time. But this happens very rarely. Most of the time, the shtick is alive and well. Not that I haven't considered other options, but I just don't find them very compelling...or fun.

One alternative to having volunteers use the software, projected so that others can work along with them, is for me to demo the software myself and have everyone do what I do. I don't like this approach for the following reasons:

- I can't focus as much on my students if I am focused on giving a demo.
- I don't wish to deprive volunteers of a "great learning opportunity."
- The audience relates better to a volunteer than to me. The volunteer will make the same mistakes, show the same hesitancy, and typically work at a pace like that of the other participants in the class, improving as they go. With my outstanding skills and knowledge, I will zip through a demonstration too quickly, making others feel inadequate and in awe of my superior capabilities and humility.

Another alternative to volunteer software users is PowerPoint. Lots and lots of PowerPoint. Here my role would not be "guide on the side" but "guide on the slide." As a mean joke for some of my training sessions, I have projected a slide labeled "Conclusion" numbered 1595. I then explained, "Oh, I accidentally advanced to the end of the deck. I'll get back to the beginning. We have much to cover." I would just see my audience collectively grimace. Don't misunderstand me. Slides can be quite effective provided:

- There are few of them.
- They are readable and not dense with information.
- They present key points that spur audience participation.
- The presenter doesn't read them aloud, bullet by bullet.
- The presenter doesn't breeze through them so quickly that no one can read them, unless the slides are boring—but then the slides shouldn't be shown at all and the presenter should be openly chastised for including boring slides that nobody wanted to see in the first place. In fact, police and citizenry in general should be authorized to issue "Bad Slide" tickets that carry a hefty fine, even greater than the fine for violating the "No Dumping" sign.

For many, slides represent a "safe" way to present. Nothing can go wrong with your presentation if all you do is read your carefully-worded slides. The presentation will be boring as hell—but free of errors or miscues. I once saw a dreadful slide show where the presenter yawned. A friend sitting next to me whispered, "My gosh, he's even boring himself."

Unless slides can trigger action, they have no appeal to me. I often ask the participants in my training classes if they would like to see some slides. They always say, quite emphatically, "*No*!" They'll gladly take the slides and read them later, but they don't want a slide-based training session. They prefer doing stuff.

Takeaway:
Beware of PowerPoint presentations that fail to engage the audience. They are PowerPointless.

Doing stuff, however, is sometimes hard when training in-person at a customer site presents physical challenges that are difficult to overcome. Among them:

- The training room is the size of a walk-in closet and there are fifty participants. The group becomes very tight knit, and I arrive having used excessive deodorant and mouthwash, hoping everyone else has too.

- There is no projector. I wave my arms around and talk a lot to the dismay of all.
- The room lights are so bright no one can see the projector. I kill the lights and we work in near total darkness. Smartphone flashlights are permitted. No candles.
- There is no internet connection. I coach participants on how to turn their smartphones into hot spots if possible, otherwise on how to expand their imaginations to pretend they have an internet connection.
- The internet connection is very weak, and we keep dropping off the Enablon applications. We work very quickly during those spurts when internet is available. I open the door, thinking irrationally that WiFi may work better if it feels welcome.
- Participants have no computers. Lots of huddling around and sharing of my laptop.
- Participants have no browser installed on their computers and must submit a special request to their IT department to install it. During the delay, while IT does the install, I tell lots of magnificent motivating

stories (like the ones in this book) and encourage participants to do the same.

- There are not enough electrical outlets for everyone's laptops and their batteries keep dying. Lots of plug sharing and quick work between charges. I curse myself for packing only edible power bars and no electric ones. And I wonder aloud, "Where is an alternative source of electricity—like Shango the Thunderer—when you need him?"
- Most of the participants scheduled to attend don't show up. I form an intimate bond with those who do. One time, no one showed. I did a lot of self-reflection and inner bonding.
- Many participants show up late or keep trickling in over a long period of time. I hone my skills in saying the same things in a variety of engaging ways. Yes, reiterating identical concepts using different verbiage. In a sense, mirroring previous statements with alternative words.
- The room is boiling hot or freezing cold and the temperature cannot be adjusted. Frequent breaks to warm up or cool down and/or fetch a change in clothes. I always wear a thick suit jacket that I can

remove to prevent heat stroke. Of course, my long underwear stays on regardless.

- There are loud disruptive sounds coming from outside the room. I try to silence the source (maybe it's someone I know), but, if not possible, I talk fast during quiet periods and otherwise quickly type my words for projection and use expressive hand signals and facial contortions.

Takeaway:
Physical deficiencies in conference/training rooms can pose substantial challenges. Use these as opportunities for improvisation, creativity, humor, and bonding with your audience.

Training, of course, was not always in-person. In fact, as web conferencing tools matured, increasingly I delivered my sessions via webinar. I love webinars for what they are, but they are distinctly different from in-person sessions. Both types of delivery have their own advantages and disadvantages. In my experience, I have seen the following pluses for webinars:

- They are much less expensive than bringing geographically dispersed participants into one physical location. Expense not only in dollars but in time and—more importantly—in hazardous emissions, the reduction of which is what Enablon is all about. This also reduces stress on the presenter (me). If participants are flown in from all over the world and put up in a nice hotel and taken away from their jobs just to come and work with me for a few days, I'd better be worth it. On the other hand, if I deliver a lame ninety-minute webinar, aside from internet costs and time (and folks could always tune me out), not much is lost.
- They force the instructor to prepare the material with much more focus, as each webinar optimally only runs from thirty minutes or less, to two hours max. After that, people lose interest. Ever wonder why most movies don't run much longer than two hours? I appreciate that it is impossible for anyone (including myself) to watch and listen to me for more than two hours and remain conscious. In some cases, for more than a few minutes.

- They can be recorded, so participants can review the material at their leisure (and repeatedly if needed and in short, merciful spurts) to reinforce the content that was discussed.
- For very small groups, already acquainted with the material but wanting to delve deeper, webinars can be an excellent vehicle for Q and A. With more participant involvement, these webinars work best.

As the webinar instructor, I pose, for all practical purposes, as a "sage on the stage" giving a performance. I am hardly a sage or a performer, and I try my best to keep my presentations short and collaborative wherever possible. Missing is the in-person face-to-face interaction, the interpretation of body language, the off-hand discussions among participants both during the session and during breaks. Some web conferencing tool salespeople try to sell their product as a replacement for in-person sessions. Web conferencing tools provide plenty of features to mimic in-person training, among them:

- Simulated "white boards" (older people like me call them "chalk boards").

- Ad hoc quiz capability, where we can test participants on a topic just covered.
- Audience "hand-raising" and ongoing survey critiquing where they can indicate whether the session is moving too fast or too slow, so the instructor can adjust accordingly on the fly.
- Easy screen sharing, so participants can show the instructor and/or others any online work they are doing related to the class.
- Webcam images of participants so we can read their facial expressions.
- Virtual class break-out "rooms" where participants can separate online from the rest of the group and carry on their discussions in private sub-groups that reconvene later with the whole class for a general discussion.

I have tried all these things. I had been coached by online training gurus while at Motorola on how to effectively use all these things. But this stuff has never worked for me. I just can't manage all these features at once. I have never been known for my multitasking ability. In fact, I have never been known for my single-tasking ability. A variation on a popular quote likely applies to me: "A fool with a (multi-feature web conferencing) tool is still a fool." I started using the webcasts, with their many instructional features, while at Motorola. I recall snatches of these sessions, all congealed in my mind, as though they are happening right now:

- I am plunged into an almost immediate frenzy. People are raising their virtual hands, their webcam faces glaring at me, virtually telling me I am moving too quickly, asking to share their screens, trying to form virtual learning groups, answering my quiz questions and wanting results, and chatting at me, all while I struggle to use my virtual pen to explain a concept on my virtual chalk board. I feel like an air-traffic controller with a dozen jumbo jets all coming in for a landing at the same time.
- Even as I gain control of the situation, I notice people are dropping off the session. Half of the dozen jumbo jets have decided to land at another airport. Participants have too many distractions staring them in the face on their computer screens—so easy to just shrink their training windows and move on to something else.

- And all these many web-learning features seem to prolong the session. The more I invite participants to share their screens, ask or answer a question, or join a virtual group, the more others lose interest as time rolls on.
- Some attendees are very passive. Saying little and participating less. I ask "George," one of my very quiet students, if he wishes to share any comments or questions with the group. No response. I ask again. A young woman finally responds, saying that "George," in fact, is a roomful of one hundred people, all watching a projection of a single computer screen. No way to get much one-on-one interaction with "George." I wonder if I have other collective participants like him. It turns out there are two more: "Susie" and "Reginald," each representing an additional roomful of people.
- And then there are the noisy participants. When unmuted to ask a question, their voices are not only loud and clear, but so are the five large dogs barking in the background or the whirling of the wind tunnel they appear to be walking through or (the worst) the

extra microphone that makes every word echo a billion times. I mute such people quickly and revert to online chat, but just as driving while texting is dangerous and illegal in most states, so is teaching while texting (at least as far as I am concerned). I avoid chatting until the session is nearly over and by then most of the chatters have bailed.

- I cannot forget the participant with the bad internet connection. "I can't hear you!" she blurts. "Wait, I'm not seeing your screen! Can everybody else see it?" Yes. "Hold on. Let me switch to another computer." A crackle. "Ah, better. I have a question." Her voice is now so soft it sounds like she is shouting at me from the moon. "I can't hear you," I respond. "Huh?" is her barely audible reply. More people are dropping off, as our imperceptible conversation is going nowhere. "Sorry," I tell her. "I can't hear you." Our banter is further destroying this already-doomed web session. I mute her in self-defense.
- As the session comes to a merciful end, curiosity gets the best of me and I display an online survey in a final attempt to spark participants' attention (for what's

left of the participants and what's left of the attention of those who are still logged in):

What did you like best about this online training session?

1. *The relevant topics being discussed*
2. *The ability to share ideas with others virtually*
3. *The hands-on practice*
4. *Other (please describe in the box below)*

- I glance at the responses. The majority is going with "Other," but most description boxes are empty. One participant writes: "Good topics." I think that was choice number one. Choice number three is a teaser—we had no true hands-on practice during the session, but three participants select it anyhow. George, Susie, and Reginald don't respond. I don't expect them to, as each roomful they represent would have to coordinate a collective vote on which answer to select.
- I unmute everyone, give a hearty thank you to all those who hung with me, including the five barking

dogs, and gracefully sign off, just as the lady with the bad internet connection whispers, "Can you hear me better now?"

I don't dislike conducting webinars. What I hate is trying to treat them like in-person sessions. I have conducted many webinars at Enablon and, in my mind at least, they were successful. My webinars are short reference demonstrations aimed at helping participants learn the software—quickly, easily, and on their own—using the webinar as a springboard.

I follow a simple format, as I am a simple knowledge manager. I demo our software applications the client wishes to learn, slowly going through the applications step-by-step and recording the session. I allow time at the end for Q and A and provide my email address for follow-up questions and some additional online references attendees can turn to besides the recording. It is essentially up to the participants to do the hands-on practice on their own.

Some smaller groups already know the software and simply wish for a web session to have their questions answered. More interaction here. But I never try to simulate an in-person interactive session. Some multitaskers, I am sure, could pull this off, using numerous web conferencing features simultaneously to dazzle the audience. But I relate more to Steve Uzzell "Multi-tasking is merely the opportunity to screw up more than one thing at a time."

I'm also realistic. I know that as soon as I say the session is being recorded, some participants will tune me out and opt to view the recording later, in their "free time." I have no problem with that. I have had rare cases where it appeared that all remote participants had tuned me out and that I was essentially speaking to an empty audience who would catch the recording later. No one was logged in to my final Q and A segment, so I made up some questions for myself and answered them brilliantly. Some clients have had me deliver multiple recorded sessions for them. I wonder whether anyone has ever binge watched those recordings. Enablon Metrics Application Season One.

The worst case is when remote participants, using a web conferencing tool, join an in-person session. We highly discourage this, but occasionally, at the client's insistence, it happens. Though microphones may be strategically placed around the classroom, remote folks often miss out on the casual conversations that occur among in-person participants. And all the remote attendees see, typically, is my screen. They miss out on ad hoc scans of fellow participants to read body language, to motion inaudibly to others, or simply to feel part of the in-person group. Finally, there is no shortening or segmentation here. Remote participants must sit through seven to eight hours, with occasional breaks and time for lunch. They can volunteer and share their screens and work with the in-person crowd, but there is still an obvious sense of isolation, which poses a major challenge.

Often, the remote attendees are practically forgotten. I must constantly remind myself that they are there and try to include them whenever possible. As a memory aid, when I know remotes will be comingled with in-persons, I try to bring a figure or picture that I set before me to remind me of the remote participants.

Once, one of my in-person students loaned me a bobble-head of Dwight Schrute from *The Office* to help remind me of a remote attendee. Whenever Dwight's little head would move, I would interact with the remote participant. Unfortunately, I grew uncomfortable with Dwight as the class progressed. His wide-open beady eyes gave me the creeps, and a few times, when I said something I thought was helpful to the group, his tiny head bobbled sideways in disagreement. During a break, I took a white paper cup, drew a smiley face on it, and put it completely over Dwight's little head. I assure you, I have never tried this with an actual real-life student.

Takeaway:

Conducting meetings/training sessions with remote participants via web-hosting tools presents its own set of challenges. Use any tool features you feel comfortable with to keep your audience engaged, keeping in mind that the experience is still not the same as being with these folks in-person.

Another learning option is e-learning. Like a recorded webinar, it can be available to students 24/7. But it is more than a passive "show" they watch. The e-learning vehicle intends not only to present content but also to allow the student to interact with that content. Some e-learning is nothing more than a glorified slide show, with intermittent stops along the way to quiz the audience to see whether they understand the slides. Some particularly nasty e-learning prevents the audience from advancing unless they score a certain percentage on these quizzes. In some, there is a final quiz, in which participants must attain a certain score to get credit for the e-learning—otherwise, they are forced to repeat the entire e-learning course.

From the Enablon perspective, e-learning is software that simulates the Enablon software, so students can interact with the simulation and thereby learn the Enablon software.

I have worked with and built e-learning programs since my middle years at Motorola. In fact, I learned how to use e-learning through e-learning. E-learning is fun, and I have built e-learning for many satisfied (at least that's what they told me) customers over the years. However, there are obvious obstacles:

- The e-learning package itself is software. If the content to be learned is also software, students must first learn the e-learning software before they can learn the actual software they are trying to learn. Sometimes, the e-learning software is harder to learn than the target software to be learned.
- Because e-learning is software, it can contain bugs, in which case the interactive simulations do not work as they should. This causes e-confusion.
- The content (software or otherwise) to be learned can change and improve rapidly. Every time it does,

the e-learning tied to that content must also be changed. What results is double effort—not only changing/improving the content, but also changing the e-learning to reflect those changes and improvements. When e-learning lags behind content, students end up learning what I like to call Content Revealing Anachronistic Particulars (CRAP).

- Clients often view working with a simulation to learn actual software as a waste of time. Why not learn directly in the actual software, instead of working with this phony simulation?

That last bullet item particularly resonates with me. From the onset of my joining Enablon, I have always claimed that if simply teaching how to use our software is my primary job as knowledge manager, then my primary goal as knowledge manager should be to eliminate my primary job. Our software should be so easy to learn, so intuitive, that formal training of any kind—in-person, webinar, e-learning—is not needed. After all, how many people take formal training to operate a smartphone? Okay, I admit some older friends (yes, myself included) do attend classes at the local public library on how to use a smartphone. But I think we go primarily for the camaraderie and the free coffee and pastries.

During my time with Enablon, I have seen our training engagements change dramatically as our software embeds more and more self-learning aids and intuitive interface functionality—even smartphone apps. In fact, a major portion of my teaching activities, regardless of format, now involves partnering with clients to determine how exactly our software best maps to their business processes.

To a large extent, I have succeeded in eliminating my primary knowledge manager job of simply teaching how to use our software and have replaced it with the job of partnering and consulting with clients to make the most of Enablon products. Using a bobble-head, preferably of someone other than Dwight Schrute, as needed.

Takeaway:

Learning tools are increasingly becoming embedded in software itself. Users are slowly moving away from asking "How do I use the software?" to "How can I use the software for the greatest benefits for myself and for my company?"

One thing that neither Motorola nor Enablon emphasized much, at least not in the customer engagements in which I was involved, was the participant evaluation. Here the audience completes a survey at the end of the session, whether it be in-person or remote training/consultation, to rate the effectiveness of the session and the instructor. Though it can gauge how happy people are, it falls short in capturing whether they have actually learned anything useful.

One of my favorite quotes comes from Henry A. Hornstein of Algoma University in Ontario, Canada, who has done extensive research in the area of SET (student evaluations of teachers): "Most of all, if the actual desire is to see improvement in teaching quality, then attention must be paid to the teaching itself, and not to the average of a list of student-reported numbers that bear at best a troubled and murky relationship to actual teaching performance."

Perhaps a more effective way to obtain feedback from participants is to ask for their opinions long after the training/consultation has occurred, to have them look back in retrospect to see whether anything useful was implemented (or even remembered) as a result of the session. But the return rate on after-the-fact surveys is abysmal. Getting 10 percent of the surveys back is viewed as outstanding.

At one time, I took such student evaluations to heart and studied them after each session to see how I might improve. But the responses were so dispersed that they never showed any clear indication of where specific improvement was needed. And often, participants' comments were contradictory or misleading.

> *"The instructor wears his ties too long."*
> *"He doesn't smile enough."*
> *"He smiles too much."*
> *"He speaks too loud."*
> *"He speaks too soft."*
> *"Brown shoes with a blue suit—really!"*
> *"He was too tolerant of that one guy in the back who was a real moron."*
> *"The class was just too short. Not enough time for me to learn."*

Most of us would agree that there is never enough time. But this comment came from a participant who arrived two hours late for each day of a five-day class and left every day two hours early. Her excuse was traffic. "That traffic was just crazy," she'd announce every morning, as she arrived just before our midmorning break. And, around 3:00 p.m., she'd be out the door, declaring, "Sorry. I must leave now. Got to beat that traffic." But apparently beating "that traffic" didn't concern her much in the morning.

"He handled that very embarrassing situation with professionalism."

This comment refers to an inadvertent slip of the tongue that turned my face tomato-red. The situation involved a participant who simply called himself Poochen. Whether this was his first name or surname was unclear, but as we progressed through the session, he indicated that he preferred to be called simply "Poo." This was awkward, and I ended up avoiding this nickname whenever possible, using gestures or just namelessly talking to him during our interactions. The last day of the session, Poochen told me he would be leaving early. We were in the middle of a class exercise, when Poochen abruptly rose and headed for the door, and that's when I said it...why I didn't say "leave" or use the full "Poochen" name, I will never know..."Do you have to go, Poo?" I followed this much too late with "...chen." By then, some wise guy in the class had already whispered loudly, "Maybe he has to go pee." I ignored the comment, smiled at Poochen, shook his hand, and wished him well. Professionalism.

"Thanks for all the help and support—especially with the cleaning advice."

Session topics did not include cleaning advice. However... James, an out-of-town participant, attended the first in-person session with curly, greying hair. When he arrived for day two, his hair was pitch black. I tried to suppress a double take when I saw him because, at first, I hardly recognized him. On a break, he approached me and whispered, "I dyed my hair. I thought I'd try it here since nobody knows me."

I was tempted to respond, "Oh, I hardly noticed." But I knew that would sound sarcastic, so I just nodded.

"I got black dye all over the shower curtain at the hotel. I wonder whether they will charge me for damages."

I knew of a cleaning solution that had worked well for me in removing difficult stains and suggested he try it. The stuff worked so well that James felt compelled to include it in his evaluation comment. I often wondered whether James retained his Elvis-black hair when he returned home.

My credence in participant evaluations disappeared once I met Jeff, the director of one of Motorola's learning organizations. Jeff referred to these evaluations as "smiles tests." He told us they meant nothing and to prove his point he conducted an experiment, which several of us were invited to watch.

A senior engineer was conducting a class for other junior engineers on some very complex content. The senior guy acted like a true "sage on the stage." He lectured on and on in a monotone voice. His encyclopedic knowledge of the subject matter was certainly impressive, but his audience struggled to take in this vast amount of information from his super dry presentations. It was a three-day class, and at the end of each day, the senior guy passed out surveys to monitor how participants were comprehending the content. Surveys for the first two days were, at best, mediocre. The audience appreciated the content and the presenter's mastery of that content but did not exhibit overflowing enthusiasm for the sessions. No one blamed the senior engineer—he was a subject-matter expert but not a teacher or consultant—and had no misconceptions that he was a good communicator.

Day three proceeded as the previous two sessions, except for the last ninety minutes of that final session when Jeff took over. He knew nothing about the content. He joked with and engaged the audience but stayed completely clear of all things technical. He was a true master at working the crowd to get a good evaluation. Occasionally, he would interject statements like: "We really appreciate your positive feedback for sessions like this, so we can continue and expand them in the future" and "I would be forever grateful if you show your support for this kind of training by evaluating it favorably." The evaluations for the last day were significantly improved over the previous two. The audience indicated they had learned and understood more (at least that's what they said). Several, in fact, went out of their way to compliment Jeff as "a fine instructor."

During my brief stint at Digital Equipment Corporation (DEC), I participated in what I judged to be a very effective training class. The instructor was knowledgeable, energetic, and, most importantly, she involved and engaged participants, so that we were driving our own learning experience. When the class concluded, mandatory teacher evaluations had been turned in, and all participants (except me) had left, I saw her in tears. "I got reamed on the evaluations," she sobbed. "The students hated me."

At DEC, evaluations were heavily weighted in instructors' performance reviews, so these bad reviews could impact her future pay increases (however small they might be anyhow) and, even worse, her job status. Totally unfair. She was a skilled instructor, a model "guide on the side." She just lacked one skill. She couldn't work the audience for good evaluations. She would say things like "Be honest when filling out the evaluations" and "We look forward to any comments and criticisms you may have so we can include them to improve the next training sessions." She might just as well have said, "It's okay to nail me to the wall." Jeff would have freaked.

I strive to be as knowledgeable as the senior engineer but as crowd-pleasing as Jeff. But I know that even if I succeed on both accounts, that still doesn't mean my students have learned anything. That's why I try to stay in contact with my students long after my training/consulting with them is over. For some, we have kept in touch for nearly a decade. They share their ups and downs with me. When I work with them, I tell them, "I am working for you, not for Enablon." I have relayed this message to Phil several times, and he has always given me a huge nod of approval. That is what learning and partnership are all about. Not some silly smiles test.

Takeaway:
The effectiveness of a learning session can only be judged by continued interaction and partnership with attendees long after the session has completed.

CHAPTER ELEVEN

MANAGING PEOPLE

During my long career at both Motorola and Enablon, I have only directly managed three people. My lack of people management experience is probably because:

- I never showed even the remotest desire to manage others, as I have enough difficulty just managing myself.

- I prefer managing non-human entities like knowledge, which can't be hostile, disagreeable, or exhibit other unpleasant human qualities.
- All the formal "housekeeping" duties associated with managing people—budget, performance reviews, ensuring team compliance with human resources policies—only put more on my plate, and I prefer a low-carb, low-formal, "housekeeping" duty diet.
- For me, the people management role was never about the role but always about the goal, and one of my goals was always not to take that role.
- As a child, leaders I had read about left a lasting impression on the type of manager I might be—Vlad the Impaler, Ivan the Terrible, Attila the Hun; I wanted no part of that scene.
- Ironically, managers I had at both Motorola and Enablon were so good that I felt I could never fill their shoes even if I wanted to (which I didn't).

Of the three people I managed, two were at Motorola and one at Enablon. The two Motorolans had been co-workers of mine when suddenly our manager decided to create another level of management and made me their manager. I knew these guys very well. They were self-starters, not in need of any real management, so my role, in additional to my previous tasks, now involved the "housekeeping" stuff, which neither of them wanted to do anyhow—and I didn't either, but what the hell.

Martin and Harry. Dan Pink could have included them in his *Drive* book.

It was past 2:00 a.m. and I was in a special audiovisual office at Motorola Schaumburg, Illinois, just finishing a webinar with folks in Singapore, who were thirteen hours ahead of me. In those early days, prime internet connections and terminals were at the office, so I could not do my sessions from home. I'd already had to shush the cleaning crew, who were noisily running their vacuum cleaners, wondering what I was still doing in the office this late. As the webinar ended, I heard a rustling behind me. The office at that point was eerily dark and quiet...but there he stood. Martin. His hair was tousled. He looked pale and had bruises near his nose and chin. He stared at me.

"Marty, what are you doing here?"

"I was in a car accident. Got shaken up. The car is drivable, but I'm not feeling well."

"You should be home, or in the hospital!"

"Wanted to come here first. I'm scheduled to teach a class tomorrow, and I don't think I am up for it. Thought I would give you a heads-up, so you'd have time to cancel the class and tell the students. Is that okay?"

I was tempted to kid him and say, "No, it's not okay. You'll have to teach that class tomorrow." Instead I said, "You could have called."

"My cell phone got trashed. I knew you'd be here. I was driving this way, so I figured I'd stop."

Thinking of your students just after a car crash. That is customer focus...to the extreme! That was Martin. I found out later that he had also interviewed for the job as knowledge manager at Enablon. But Phil's badass interviewing technique really irritated him, so I ended up with the job. When Martin found out, he wrote a gushing letter to Phil, telling him how great I was and how lucky Enablon was to be hiring me. Had Phil known the car crash story, it could have been Martin instead of me writing this book...except the title would have been different since Martin is a lot younger than I am, and the writing, of course, would not have been as magnificent.

Harry had a most compelling start to life. He was the youngest person to have escaped the holocaust, having been born on a ship that was escaping the Nazis in World War II. I suspect this brush with death, even at an extremely early age, instilled him with an extraordinary love of life. Whenever anyone greeted Harry with the standard "How are you?" his response was always "Outstanding" or "Fantastic." He was the most upbeat person I have ever met on the job.

One day Harry confided in me that he had been diagnosed with early-onset Alzheimer's disease. He told me about it with such humor and grace that I was totally awed by his bravery. "What exactly did the doctor say regarding your memory loss?" I asked him.

He couldn't help but tap into an old joke. "He told me to pay him in advance."

Harry had been noticing his failing memory gradually, like when he forgot where he had parked his car. But eventually the situation progressed to the point where, when consulting with a group of Motorola engineers, he could not remember, after lunch, what he had been discussing with them that morning. Yet he was extremely clever and was able to hide his condition. When someone asked him a question about something of which he had no recollection, he would respond, "Well, what do you think?" or he would turn to another member of the group and ask for their feedback. He so involved others, in fact, that they learned much from their encounters with Harry and demonstrated their enhanced skills on the job. His condition, ironically, totally diminished his "sage on the stage" persona, making him a true guide and observer and empowering those with whom he worked to truly drive their own learning.

Harry's story has a happy ending. He was misdiagnosed. His memory issues, it turned out, were the result of one too many falls while ice skating and roller blading. He had suffered numerous concussions, the most recent of which finally triggered his memory loss. But after several months of more moderate activity and avoidance of head injury, his memory eventually returned. The episode, however, served to highlight for all of us that even if we do know something, we can help others by letting them take a bigger role in managing their learning experiences. Harry eventually retired to the West Coast, where, I was happy to learn, he became an obsessive kayaker, where there is diminished chance of further head bumps. As going-away gifts, I bought him a set of paddles and, as a further precaution, a kayak helmet. I sincerely wanted him never to forget me.

The next three paragraphs will, at first, seem an extraneous digression. But bear with me. They relate (as you will see if you stick with me) to Mike, the only Enablonian whom I ever actually managed. Of course, as you read on, you may decide that the next three paragraphs really are extraneous digression.

In my very early working days, before either Motorola or Enablon, I had been a middle school teacher. That was before computer science was even recognized as a degree program in any university. Yes, I am that old.

I also have an affinity toward those associated with bowling. I come from a bowling family. My mom and dad both worked for a bowling supply company and met while bowling in the company-sponsored league. As a child, I loved to bowl and admired professional bowlers. Every Saturday afternoon during winter, the PBA (Professional Bowlers Association) tours would be broadcast on ABC TV, with the legendary bowling announcer Chris Schenkel. I was glued to the screen. My favorite bowler was Chicago's own Carmen Salvino. In my later years at Motorola, I had an amazing, motivating manager named Corinne. Occasionally, she would mention, off-hand, that her father was involved in bowling. Then one day, during a meeting, she said exactly who her father was. My jaw dropped. I was in shock for the remainder of the meeting. Carmen Salvino. Corinne had gone by her married name, so I never made the connection. I was working for the daughter of Carmen Salvino, my bowling hero from childhood. How cool was that? At one point, I was even able to meet him and get his autograph, to add to my collection of Bob Galvin and Dennis Ritchie. As I suspected, Carmen was not only a superstar bowler, he was a superstar person.

Once, during a meeting with Corinne, another co-worker mentioned the name of a Motorola contact, Joe Joseph. Corinne and I looked at each other and smiled. We knew this wasn't *the* Joe Joseph—the famous pro bowler with the ultra-smooth release. Corinne and I shared a lot of bowling trivia that few others at Motorola knew. She had lived it, accompanying her dad to many of the tournaments; I had watched it via Chris Schenkel.

Back to Mike. Knowledge management work was growing, and I needed help. When I interviewed Mike for a position on my team, I was tempted to use the "Yes, but...," hard-to-please, Phil Tesler technique, to see how Mike would respond under pressure. But I couldn't do it. He immediately came across as such a nice guy. And he was passionate about preserving the environment. And he had been a schoolteacher (like me). And he had previously worked for the same bowling supply company where my parents had worked. His job had been to teach bowling proprietors how to use his company-supplied software to manage their bowling centers. This was what especially captured my attention.

These bowling proprietors owned the bowling alleys. Their livelihood was based largely on how well this software performed and how well they understood it. Mike had the ultimate demanding customer and he had thrived on the job until, like me, along came the great recession of 2008 and folks didn't have a lot of extra money to invest in bowling. How could I not hire this guy? Angela liked him too, though she had not been a schoolteacher nor had any family history in bowling. I didn't even ask him whether he spoke French (which, it turned out, he didn't).

Martin, Harry, and Mike—three motivated guys who, though they formally reported to me, I never tried to manage. They had the self-determination and smarts to manage themselves. I served, at most, as a "guide on the side."

Takeaway:
Most employees don't require management. They require partnership.

CHAPTER TWELVE

CHANGES

Heraclitus said, "There is nothing permanent except change." And he knew this firsthand, as his quote was often changed to "Nothing is permanent except change" or "No thing is permanent but change." As my time progressed with Enablon, I could notice changes in myself. The older I got (and I was old to start with), I developed a new perspective on time and an acknowledgement of my own physical limitations. Increasingly, I wanted to spend more time enjoying the basic and fundamental joys of life—spending more time with family and friends, taking long leisurely walks, exercising more, sleeping more, spending more time reading, writing, and reflecting, and watching old *Monk* episodes I had missed.

I also noticed that my stamina for delivering numerous consecutive interactive sessions, especially when they involved travel, was faltering. Though I was sensing my decline for quite a while, it became obvious to me during onsite training for a customer with several locations scattered throughout remote portions of Mexico.

One site was so remote that we reached it from Mexico City via a client-owned private airplane, landing on a dirt runway. Our camp, consisting of small apartments, was a half-hour drive to the actual worksite up in the mountains. Because I would be delivering training at the actual worksite, I was required to wear PPE (personal protective equipment), which consisted of a hard hat, protective goggles, a bright orange safety vest, and steel-toed boots, all supplied by the client, who had taken my measurements in advance to ensure everything would fit.

Each morning, at 6:30 a.m., in pitch dark, with our PPE attire, we boarded the convoy of vans, escorted by armed guards who rode in a lead truck, in a truck in the middle of the convoy, and in one at the tail end. My audience spoke little English (and my Spanish was as lacking as my French), but the client had arranged for a translator named Ernesto to accompany me.

"Why the guards?" I asked him, noticing the helmets, bulky (probably bullet-proof) vests, and huge machine guns of the guys in the front truck immediately preceding us. There was no doubt that these folks were mercenaries.

"Just a precaution. Against bandits coming down from the hills and stealing."

"Stealing what?"

"Us. Kidnappers. Then they hold us for ransom."

Pleasant thought for an early morning ride. I gulped.

"Just a precaution," he smiled. "Nothing to worry about."

Bouncing up and down as the van sped along the rough road up steep hills in the dark protected by guys with big guns, I was beginning to feel like Indiana Jones. I hoped this wouldn't be my last crusade.

We joined the work site just as a mandatory general meeting was in progress. We were asked to attend. The meeting was held in what looked like a large, open-air storage building. Workers—probably over a hundred of them, I guessed—were seated on long benches, while the presenter showed

PowerPoint graphs and narrated by microphone in Spanish. We had come late and so were standing against the pillars of an open wall. I was wearing my hard hat, safety goggles and vest, and, of course, my steel-toed boots. I could barely see the graphs and had no idea of what the speaker was saying. It was very hot. I seemed to be sweating more than normal, probably due to the vest. And I was breathing harder. Then, suddenly, I was out. Only for a few seconds. I could see others rushing toward me to break my fall. They escorted me to an ambulance, where I was placed on a stretcher and driven a very short distance to the infirmary, where I got the full treatment from the medical team. They hooked me up to an oxygen tank. They checked my pulse, blood pressure, and heart rate. They gave me an electrocardiogram.

They spoke little English, but, thankfully, Ernesto had accompanied me in the ambulance. "They say your heart rate is low," he explained. "They want to give you a stimulant."

"No, no. That's okay. My heart rate is always low. I run a lot." By now, I was feeling fine, although a bit embarrassed as my pants were all dirty at the knees from my fall. This experience was quite stimulating in itself. No need for chemicals.

It occurred to me that what had just happened was the type of thing that typically got logged into our incident management software. I'll bet the medical team had logged it. Probably under the title: "*Viejo pero guapo americano se desmaya.*"

I sat around the infirmary a bit longer, drank some water, and chatted with Ernesto, who seemed preoccupied with Donald Trump. It was 2016 and we were in the midst of the presidential debates between Hillary and the Donald. Ernesto was full of questions: What did I think of Trump? What was he really like (as if I knew)? What did other Americans think of Trump? Have I ever stayed at a Trump resort? Did I ever see him in person? Did I think that was his real hair? Was it really orange? Did I watch him much on TV? Had I seen any of the debates?

"Ernesto, why are you so interested in Trump?"

His eyes opened wide and he declared, "Because I am Trump."

Okay, so I'm still fully dressed in PPE in an infirmary somewhere in remote Mexico having just passed out in the dirt, and the only person I can communicate with is a crazy translator who thinks he is Donald Trump. Should I ask him if Melania came with him? Or maybe are Ivanka and Jared in the vicinity?

Ernesto could read the "you are nuts" look in my eyes. "No, you don't understand. I am Trump on television."

Was this guy fantasizing about hosting *The Apprentice*?

Ernesto continued. "During the debates, I am Trump. I translate his words on Spanish television. So, during the debates, I try to act like him as much as possible to be convincing, to talk like he would talk—only in Spanish."

I'd bet Ernesto was getting quite practiced in saying "*mujer desagradable*" and "Hillary *torcida*" with that unique Trump inflection.

Enough of Trump. I was feeling much better, and, with Ernesto's help, convinced the medical team that I could leave the infirmary and walk to the training room to begin the session, which went surprisingly well. Participants were truly engaged, and we interacted better than I had hoped—largely due to Ernesto's gusto in translating.

"I apologize," Ernesto told me. "I am afraid that my television persona may have carried over into my translation of what you are saying.

"How is that?" I asked him.

"One of the students told me that some of your expressions sound like Donald Trump." *Believe me*, I hoped the students—these *incredible men and women*—did not think that this *great guy*, Ernesto, was making me sound like the Donald. Me sounding like Trump? That was an alternative fact.

My fainting incident continued to bother me. It was the first time I had ever passed out on the job. Even though I later learned that it was not uncommon for new visitors to the work site to faint due to the sudden increase in elevation, I was beginning to doubt my physical stamina. Did this mean I would no longer be able to climb Mt. Everest? Not that I had the slightest interest in doing so, but the possible limitation bothered me.

My flight back to Mexico City in the client-owned private airplane only compounded my concern when I became air sick—also for the first time in my life. True, the plane was jouncing around in the air a bit more than I was used to, and the other passengers were all repeatedly making signs of the cross (I even spotted one rosary), but I had never gotten sick from a plane ride before. I was slowing down, losing momentum.

I shared my concerns with Phil and Angela. "I don't think I can continue working at this pace. I am wearing down physically, and I am beginning to realize that I need more time for myself, for a better work-life balance."

I was expecting a "Yes, but..." answer from them both. "Yes, but this is not possible right now. If you insist on reducing your work time, we will have to replace you."

Instead, Angela and Phil conferred, and the response I got was: "Whatever you want. You can work as a contractor or remain an Enablon employee part-time. Set the hours you think are reasonable."

Talk about autonomy! We quickly came to an agreement. I would remain an Enablon employee. My hours would be more flexible, and I could work mostly from home when my presence wasn't absolutely needed at the Willis Tower. For me, this was an ideal situation. I was growing more satisfied with my job by having more time to enjoy life overall. As Heather Schuck wrote in *The Working Mom Manifesto*: "You will never feel truly satisfied by work until you are satisfied by life."

Another huge change occurred a year later. Angela called and, in an emotion-filled voice, told me she would be leaving Enablon. As much as she loved the company, she needed time away, and a part-time arrangement like mine was simply not enough for her. There were tears and reflections and recollections of fond memories during that call. It was a very sad day for me. I especially remembered our fun team events in Paris—the Voca People, the Seine cruise on the *Bateau Mouche,* the group dinner at the quaint bistro. Oddly, even the infamous and mysterious Rodrigo came to mind and how calmly Angela had handled what could have been a disastrous situation.

Angela's enthusiasm, her motivating management style, her customer focus, and her genuine concern for others so embodied the Enablon spirit that it was hard to say goodbye. We promised to stay in touch, at least via email and social media, which we do. Though she is gone, the spark that she brought to Enablon, and to Enablon knowledge management, continues to shine and thrive. Angela was much more than a manager; she was a dear friend and a leader.

Steven Covey's quote is so appropriate in describing Angela's leadership style: "Management is efficiency in climbing the ladder of success; leadership determines whether the ladder is leaning against the right wall." As I stumbled up the ladder—not far up as I was always worried about falling off—I was continually reassured by Angela's thoughtfulness and by her strategic positioning of that ladder.

One thing I noticed about Angela and the other Enablon managers was that they never seemed to let anger or frustration get the best of them. They kept cool, focused, and in control. I recall having delivered a web-based presentation to a large audience, so large that they were automatically muted to prevent background sound interference (from dogs barking, wind tunnels, microphone echoes, and other miscellaneous noises). But I had forgotten to unmute myself during the session.

I didn't check the webinar tool chat box until the very end of the session. The chat box was loaded with messages: "No sound." "Can't hear you." "Audio trouble." And on and on. I felt so stupid. I had gotten so carried away in talking—for an hour—that I had never bothered to try to interact with my audience. I had been talking to myself. A stooge on the stage. When I told Angela, I expected at least a tinge of anger on her part. But no.

Her response. "Not a big deal. So, you'll have to reschedule the session and do it again. Don't worry about it. Shit happens."

I was lucky to have never been the brunt of a manager's explosive anger. Phil's "Yes, but..." interview was not angry, just purposefully irritating. I did see a manager's furious flare-up second-hand while at Motorola. My friend Martin and I, who at that time were co-workers and in the throes of a management change, had been at an onsite project and were returning home. Having just dropped off our rental car, we were on the shuttle to the airport. One fellow passenger on the shuttle was loud and extremely obnoxious. He complained that the shuttle was late, that it was slow and dirty and unbearably hot, that the overall service at the car rental was terrible, that the cars were junk, and that the car rental workers didn't know what they were doing. Martin and I looked at each other, then at the irate passenger. "I think I know that guy," Martin whispered to me.

I nodded. I recognized him too. He was our new manager. He had been pointed out to us by some of our colleagues before the trip, but we hadn't been introduced to him yet, so he didn't know who we were. He must have been visiting the same client site, but we hadn't seen him until that point. "Do you think this is the right time to introduce ourselves to him?"

Martin winced. "No way."

Our irate manager was at the front of the shuttle, and we were seated toward the back and decided to complete the ride incognito, hiding our faces as much as possible. He was also on the same flight back to Chicago but sat up front in first class while we coached it. The organization changed again shortly after our shuttle experience, so our irate manager wasn't our manager for long. And, to be fair, he was an okay manager, but thoughts of his explosive behavior on that shuttle always made us a bit wary of him and our relationship was never as close as it could have been. I am convinced he had no idea that we had witnessed his rent-a-car outburst. I felt compelled to compose a brief "Ode to the Rent-a-Burst," which is hardly a candidate for *Poetry Magazine*, but which I present here for your muddled and befuddled enjoyment.

A manager's behavior should be subtle
No outbursts on the airport shuttle
Or you might face employee rebuttal
And that could create quite a muddle
Causing you to ask who will or what'll
Avoid a situation that could befuddle.

When Angela told me she was leaving, I admit that my first thoughts were self-serving. Who is going to replace her and how will this affect me? All Enablon managers I had seen had been cool, calm, people-focused, and motivating. Granted, I hadn't ridden with any of them on an airport shuttle. I feared that there might be one well-hidden manager from hell among the Enablon management pool and that it would be my misfortune to end up reporting to that one.

But my fears were unwarranted. Caroline, who, like Angela, was also headquartered in Paris, became my new manager and proved to be an absolute delight. Unlike Angela, Caroline was not a knowledge manager, but an extremely technical software architect who focused on Enablon's overall software infrastructure and support. Caroline liked to talk about very technical topics and so did I, except my very technical concentration had been years earlier and the half-life of what I had learned had diminished my expertise to practically nothing. Still, I enjoyed our conversations and even understood tiny fragments of them.

Caroline and Angela studied from the same playbook of management—manager, leader, friend, and motivator, with a contagious passion for Enablon purpose and technology. In fact, rumor has it that an American singer/songwriter was so impressed with Caroline's work ethic that he dedicated a song just to her. That's right. Neil Diamond. "Sweet Caroline." Granted, others have said the song's inspiration was John F. Kennedy's daughter, Caroline. Whatever. I realize that rumor is on shaky ground because when "Sweet Caroline" was released in 1969, my manager Caroline had not yet been born. Still, I'd at least like to believe that if Neil knew of Enablon manager Caroline, he'd *re*-dedicate the song to her.

I think Phil, like Angela and me, was also beginning to re-examine work-life balance. One day when I came into the office, he commented on how much younger I appeared now that I was taking more time for myself (he was either being kind or not looking directly at my face) and that he, too, Mr. Workaholic, was beginning to re-evaluate how he spent his time. He had even taken up jogging—and 5K and 10K races, no less!

In 2015, Dan and Marc Vogel and Phil announced that they were considering "investors" in Enablon. I considered investors to be individual people, probably rich people or groups of rich people, who would loan money to Enablon to help us expand. Since Enablon is French-based, I expected the rich people to be primarily French or at least well-known in France, maybe someone like Bernard Arnault, François Pinault, or Gad Elmaleh. Or maybe even Michael Jordan, as he had played basketball in Paris during a Chicago Bulls visit and was quite popular there.

I was wrong.

In mid-2016, an abrupt, all-hands Enablon meeting was called. The "investors" had emerged. But "buyer" was a better word. Wolters Kluwer, it was announced, had acquired Enablon. Who or what was Wolters Kluwer? I had never heard of it. At first, I thought it was an investor person, named Walter Kluger. But I soon became acquainted with Wolters Kluwer, a huge worldwide information services company, headquartered in the Netherlands, whose origins date back as far as 1836 (well before I was born). Hardly a young start-up. And many of my friends had heard of Wolters Kluwer, as well. Some had even tried to get a job there. As I learned more about the acquisition, I had more thoughts of déjà vu.

- Four-Phase Systems was twelve years old when it was acquired by the much-larger Motorola. Enablon was four years older (as in Four-Phase)—sixteen—when it was acquired by the much-larger Wolters Kluwer.
- When I was hired by Four-Phase Systems (which had already been acquired by Motorola), one of my wife's two uncles worked for Motorola. When Enablon was acquired by Wolters Kluwer, my wife's other uncle had worked for Wolters Kluwer.
- Motorola had purchased Four-Phase Systems for approximately $250 million US dollars. Wolters

Kluwer purchased Enablon for approximately €250 million Euros.

- Both new owners shared the same passion as their acquisitions. With Motorola and Four-Phase, it was a passion for improving life through computer processing technology. With Wolters Kluwer and Enablon, it is focus on risk management, regulatory compliance, and sustainability.
- The new owners, Motorola and Wolters Kluwer, introduced enhanced processes and resources that helped Four-Phase and Enablon, respectively, better compete in an aggressive market and better serve the needs of their customers and employees.
- Some really stretch comparisons here but humor me: The “W” in Wolters, when placed upside-down, looks like the “M” in Motorola, and vice versa. The “E” in Enablon immediately precedes the “F” in Four-Phase. Both Motorola and Wolters Kluwer have four (as in Four-Phase) syllables.
- As founder and CEO, Lee Boysel, departed Four-Phase as the acquisition completed, so too did Dan, Marc, and Phil, who all made plans to eventually depart Enablon.

The last bullet point was the saddest for me because I truly liked and respected the Vogel brothers and especially their friend Phil. Dan was the first to leave after a six-month transition period. Marc followed, about six months after that. Marc, who originally was Angela's boss, emailed me a good-bye response that included: "Although as you said we didn't work much together I have heard only good things about you. In addition, I have always enjoyed your sense of humour." It was gratifying to note that someone enjoyed my sense of humor (spelled in the elegant British style "humour"). In fact, it was gratifying that someone (besides myself) even noticed that I had a sense of humor.

Phil stayed on the longest.

Our internal seminar for all North America-based Enablonians, held early in 2018, proved to be his last hurrah. On that day, we all dressed like Phil—baseball cap, dark pullover, dark jeans (tight for those of us who chose to wear them). As part of the seminar tradition, awards were given to employees for accomplishments throughout the year. I hate public award ceremonies for the following reasons:

- They tend to be qualitative, not quantitative, and that means some judge or judges decide the "winner" and that's where subjectivity (and sometimes politics) enters in. So, they are not fair. Want proof? The Oscars. The Grammys. The Golden Globe Awards. The Emmys. The Tonys. And all the dozens of music-related awards. Beauty pageants. The All-Star Game (name any sport). Strictly quantitative awards, I can live with. For example, if you win the race because you had the fastest time—please take your award. You deserve it.

- If the intent is to motivate award candidates by providing an incentive, the actual result is the exact opposite. For every award winner announced in public, there are at least ten others (usually more) who think they should have won and deep-down feel that they were screwed by the "awards committee." Just watch the faces of the Oscar nominees as soon as the winner is announced. Marvel at the fake smiles and applause of the losers, who are truly tapping into their acting skills.
- I know what you're thinking. One of the reasons I hate public awards is because: I never won one. But that's not true. Surprisingly, I have, and I always felt very awkward about it. When asked to say some-

thing, I would imitate my favorite acceptance speech (the shortest, given by Patty Duke, who won the Best Supporting Actress Oscar for *The Miracle Worker* in 1963): "Thank you."

But in 2018, at Phil's farewell Enablon internal seminar, I had won an award. Despite everything I have just said to bash public awards, I was happy to approach the stage and accept the prize for two reasons.

1. I was accepting an award along with a co-worker on the KM team, whose name was also Tom and who had done fantastic work, which I had repeatedly witnessed. Definitely an award-winning performance that, I was convinced, would pass any quantitative test. So I was happy to accompany the other Tom, where, I hoped, the focus would be on him (rightly so), with me tagging along as a member of the supporting cast.
2. When I got the mic for a thank-you speech, it gave me the opportunity this time, not to do my Patty Duke impression, but to deliver a heartfelt public thanks

to Phil for his help and leadership to me personally and to all of Enablon.

The day was emotional. It ended with a big hug from Phil. He would move on to a special consulting position at Wolters Kluwer while also working on a new venture to help technology companies achieve global positive social and environmental impact. But, as of this writing, I have not seen him since.

As a side note, I will be happy to approach the awards stage again, when this book formally receives public accolades—the Nobel Prize in Literature, the Pulitzer Prize, the National Book Award, the Hallucinating Fantasy Award, and countless others.

Takeaway:
Continual change is all around us. Adapt. Enjoy fond memories. Keep fresh the key lessons learned from what was and apply them to what is and what will be. But realize that constant change is the only thing that doesn't change.

Phil left Enablon North America in good hands. His successor as CEO was Chris Joseph. Prior to Phil's departure, Chris had served as co-CEO with Phil, so Chris's change of role was carefully planned and smoothly executed.

Earlier I mentioned that what makes a CEO truly great is that he/she appreciates the importance of others, regardless of how insignificant or lowly they are in the organization, like me. And because of this, most employees have stories about their interaction with the CEO. It didn't take long for me to experience my own Chris Joseph stories.

I was flying to Houston to participate in a local Enablon SPF (Sustainable Performance Forum) for our clients in the Houston area. As I deplaned, I noticed that several of my Enablon colleagues—who were also participating in the SPF—were on the same flight. One of them was Chris. I had met him briefly, but we had never talked for any length. Our Enablon group gathered at the terminal and planned to share a ride to the hotel where the SPF was being held. Everyone had checked luggage and had to go to baggage claim except Chris and me. I always travel light (and wrinkled) and learned that he did too.

"Why don't you and I just go ahead?" he suggested. "The others can share a ride once they get their luggage."

That was fine with me, and so we ended up having plenty of time to talk one-on-one during the long cab ride to the hotel. I learned that we both had sons in the military, and, as I think anyone who is associated with our armed forces knows, there is a strong bond among military families. But even had there not been this connection, Chris was easy to connect with. During the entire ride, he never once brought up business. He kept the conversation on the personal level throughout and seemed genuinely interested in me—old, insignificant person that I am. The sign of a great CEO. I only regret that I didn't ask him (and still haven't asked him as of this writing) whether he was somehow related to Joe Joseph, that ever-so-smooth professional bowler, whom, like Carmen Salvino, I marveled at as a kid. With my affinity toward all people associated with bowling, I would like to think so.

At another SPF in Chicago, Chris thought it would be a fun idea for those of us participating in a segment of the conference where we would answer customer questions to wear more casual, unique attire—like colorful polo shirts or T-shirts and/or baseball caps emblazoned with large letters saying "Enablon Genius" or "Keep Enablon Weird" (referring to the "Keep Austin Weird" movement—that later spread to other cities—to promote small local businesses).

I thought the whole idea was weird and said so in an email that eventually got to Chris. In my email, I referenced (among several sources) the Career Trend website, which notes: "Dressing professionally can make you feel better about yourself. Comfy sweats and T-shirts can create a relaxed, I-don't-care kind of attitude. When you dress up in a suit, you tend to stand straighter and project more confidence, which people will respond to positively."

Now I know this doesn't apply to everyone. Phil was always clad in a black pullover and jeans. And Ron could easily get away with his puffy shirt. But I need all the help I can get, so whenever engaging with clients, I always wear a suit and tie, unless they specifically tell me otherwise, as in the remote sites of Mexico.

At any rate, the "Enablon Genius"/"Keep Enablon Weird" casual attire idea got nixed. The morning of the first day of SPF Chicago, Chris entered the lobby of the main conference hall and made a beeline right toward me. "I was wrong about casual clothes," he told me. "Thanks for your very detailed, convincing email."

How many CEOs would admit, outright, that they were wrong while a lowly employee (like me) was right? Another sign of a great CEO. As he spoke, I just felt oh-so-lucky that I was wearing a suit and tie and that I hadn't reversed my strong opinions on attire and showed up at the SPF in an "Ain't I smart" T-shirt with cut-off jeans that had "Seat of Wisdom" or "Yes, Butt" across the rear.

As of this writing, I am still working for Enablon and loving it—and in hopes of new adventures to come. However, by the time you read this, more changes may have occurred. I might be slowing down more, losing more momentum. Who knows what could be happening?

- I may have begun serious study of French and Spanish and be teaching these languages at a local college (or, more realistically, preschool).
- I may have reunited with Ernesto and resumed sounding like a Spanish Donald Trump, though I know this sounds like fake news.
- I may have co-authored a coffee table book with my old acquaintance Mr. Bartholome.
- The elusive and treacherous Rodrigo and I may have finally crossed paths, *mano a mano*, and by force I

may have recovered the stolen down payment and returned it safely to Enablon, to the cheers of honest citizens worldwide (after deducting a substantial recovery fee).

- I may have gone on to pen more award-winning books like this one, as well as screen and theater and musical adaptations of my works—or at least have dreamed of doing this while snoozing on the couch during a binge session of *Monk* reruns.

You can be sure that whatever I end up doing will be aligned with my definition for success at that time. And regardless of my status, I am confident that I will never forget the marvelous experiences and people described in this book. These memories are truly sustainable. And why shouldn't they be? After all, so many of them have stemmed from Enablon, *the* sustainable software company.